# TEACHING CONTENT
## TO ENGLISH
## LANGUAGE LEARNERS

### STRATEGIES FOR
### SECONDARY SCHOOL
### SUCCESS

Jodi Reiss

Longman

**Teaching Content to English Language Learners:
Strategies for Secondary School Success**

Pearson Education, 10 Bank Street, White Plains, NY 10606

Reviewers: **Heidi Ballard**, University of California at Berkeley, Henry M. Gunn High
School, Palo Alto, CA; **Lynore M. Carnuccio**, Educational Consultant, Yukon, OK;
**Kristin Grayson**, University of Central Oklahoma; **Kathleen Anderson Steeves**,
The George Washington University, Washington, DC

Editorial director: Sherry Preiss
Acquisitions editor: Laura Le Dréan
Development manager: Paula H. Van Ells
Development editor: Tara Maldonado
Production editor: Lynn Contrucci
Marketing manager: Joe Chapple
Senior manufacturing buyer: Nancy Flaggman
Cover design: Pat Wosczyk
Cover photo: Dimitri Vervitsiotis/Digital Vision Ltd.
Text composition: Laserwords Pvt. Ltd.
Text font: 10/12 Palatino
Illustrations: Jill Wood

**Library of Congress Cataloging-in-Publication Data**

Reiss, Jodi.
Teaching content for English language learners / Jodi Reiss.
p. cm.
Includes bibliographical references.
ISBN 0-13-152357-0
1. English language—Study and teaching—Foreign speakers. 2. Interdisciplinary
approach in education. I. Title.
PE1128.A2R457 2005
428'.007--dc22

2004017689

Printed in the United States of America
2 3 4 5 6 7 8 9 10—VHO—08 07 06 05

# TEACHING CONTENT

## TO ENGLISH
## LANGUAGE LEARNERS

# Contents

# Preface

This book is written for the middle and high school math, science, and social studies teachers who find themselves responsible for the academic success of the English language learners in their classrooms. You, as highly accomplished teachers in your own disciplines, are unfamiliar with the basics of second language learning (of course!). You have attended state-mandated courses, workshops, and presentations that dealt with the issues of teaching language learners. And what you have ended up with are lists of *shoulds*—you *should* make your teaching more accessible; you *should* speak more simply; you *should* give less complex assignments; you *should* increase class participation. What you lack are the specifics for actually putting these excellent theoretical principles into effect. The goal of this text is to fill those gaps.

This book is light on theory, jargon, and technical terminology. Its purpose is to provide you with practical, easy-to-incorporate ideas that fit right in with the techniques and activities you currently use in your classrooms.

The inspiration for this book came as a direct result of my years of teaching Masters' level courses at the College of Education at Florida International University. Working with teachers showed me the burdens and challenges that today's teachers regularly face. Teachers always need more time and more resources. One of my goals for this book was to provide immediately usable ideas that would not place additional burdens on teachers' time or workload.

Even more saliently, my work with teachers filled me with awe for their love and dedication to their chosen profession. They wanted to be the best teachers they could possibly be. They actively sought solutions to issues they faced. They welcomed suggestions and delighted in reporting those that were successful. Simply stated, they loved finding and sharing ideas that worked.

And so this book is written to share with you a multitude of solutions that work with the English language learners in your content classes. The strategies presented here are designed to enrich your daily activities of teaching in ways that will be more effective for your language-learning students. You will not have to change the way you teach—every strategy in this book can be easily incorporated into your current practices. The many strategies for teaching and testing offer you versatile and effective options; use those that fit your teaching style and subject matter. The choice is yours.

One last thing I learned from working with teachers is this: successful teachers are happy teachers. It is my hope that the strategies in this text will add to your pleasure in teaching. I wish you great success!

Jodi Reiss

# PART I

# Teaching in Multicultural Classrooms: An Introduction

# CHAPTER 1

# The Challenge

---

**Case Study—Mr. Elkind's Classroom**

Mr. Elkind teaches social studies in middle school. In every one of his daily classes he has some students who are in the process of learning English. He and his fellow teachers often talk about the growing number of English language learners (ELLs) in their classes.

Mr. Elkind and his colleagues are teachers who care about their students and what they are learning. In the teachers' lounge and at lunch, conversations often turn to discussions of ideas to motivate their students, to raise their levels of interest and participation, and ultimately, to increase their learning. They talk a great deal about the situation with their English language learners, who, they all agree, are bright, motivated, focused, and respectful. These teachers recognize the need to facilitate the learning experience for their ELLs and to get them more involved in their classrooms, but they're not at all sure about how to do it.

Mr. Elkind is particularly concerned because social studies knowledge depends so heavily on reading and research skills. The English language learners in his classes rarely participate in class discussions and activities. He tries to call on them only for what he thinks are the "easy" questions:

- Who won the Civil War—the North or the South? Shihan, want to give it a try?
- Luis, can you tell us what year the war ended?
- Asma, what was the name of the period that followed the end of the Civil War?

Shihan, Luis, and Asma, upon hearing their names, look uncomfortable. Mr. Elkind's questions are almost always met with silence and downcast eyes. Nothing he has tried has worked very well, and he is becoming increasingly troubled. Helping these students learn has become an important issue to him.He thinks back to his early years of teaching and remembers many of the challenges he faced, but he doesn't recall this as being one of them.

---

Mr. Elkind's memory is accurate. Growth of minority populations is a nation-wide phenomenon, and the rate of that growth is increasing year by year. In the twelve years from 1991 to 2002, the number of English language learners in public schools, kindergarten through twelfth grade, rose 95% to 4.75 million. Total public school enrollment during those same years increased only 12%. In 2004, the number of English language learners attending U.S. public schools exceeded 5 million.

Every state in the nation has felt the effects of this growth. School districts, even the smallest ones, are facing the challenge of developing programs and services to help these students learn English as well as math, science, and social studies.

## LEARNING ENGLISH: PROGRAMS AND GOALS

Approaches to instruction vary among schools, school districts, and counties, but the primary objective of all school programs for nonnative speakers is the same: to teach them to understand, speak, read, and write English. In the past, when non-English-speaking students were concentrated in fewer cities and states, the immersion method of learning English was the prevalent approach. Non-English speakers were simply placed in regular classes and were expected to learn English and content subjects along with the other students. This approach was decidedly less a "method" of language instruction and more a "sink-or-swim" technique. In those times, some language learners swam and some sank—but all of them suffered.

Today's approaches take a wider view of both linguistic theory and pedagogical practice. The language learners as well as the language learning process are now taken into account in decisions on how to structure school programs. Many school districts use a combination of program types depending on grade level and the numbers of students involved.

In pull-out programs, English language learners are taken out of their regular classrooms for one or two hours a day to work with special teachers for instruction in English, reading, and language arts. In push-in programs, the special English language teacher comes to the language learners' class and teaches them as a group within their own classroom. In schools where English language learners are mainstreamed, the regular English or language arts teacher is responsible for meeting the special instructional needs of these students.

Some schools group their English language learners in special classes designated as *self-contained ESOL* (English for Speakers of Other Languages) or *bilingual* classrooms. A smaller number of schools have developed programs involving a highly structured *sheltered instruction* approach. The main objective of all of these programs, regardless of type, is to develop English language proficiency in those students who speak languages other than English.

## IN CONTRAST: THE FOCUS OF CONTENT LEARNING

While today's programs have come a long way from the "sink-or-swim" approach of past times, few of them address the issue of content learning for English language learners. In middle schools and high schools, ELLs are usually placed in regular classes for social studies, math, and science, as well as other subjects. Instruction in those subject areas falls squarely upon the shoulders of the regular content teacher—you—and, like Mr. Elkind and his colleagues, you may be searching for ways to make your content more accessible for these students.

You may feel that your regular instructional practices are not working very effectively with English language learners at the beginner or intermediate level. You may even be questioning whether students who are in the process of developing English language skills can possibly understand and learn the content you are trying to teach. The good news is that they can, indeed—it will take only a little extra effort on your part. You can increase the success of your English language learners by understanding how to make the *language* of your content easier to access for these students.

Because you are a content teacher, your area of knowledge and expertise is in the content itself. Teacher training, workshops, conferences, readings, and experience have expanded your knowledge base and your ideas for more effective teaching techniques and activities. Compare this focus with the focus of the language arts or English teacher, whose subject matter is the *English language* itself. In these classrooms, the content focuses on the continued development of the skills of language: reading, writing, speaking, and listening.

In math, science, and social studies classrooms, little, if any, attention is paid to language. Language is simply the *medium* of instruction. It exists only as the means to deliver the content itself. Now, in today's changing teaching environment, content teachers must shift their perspective to include strategies that consider the medium as well as the content of instruction in order to reach and teach the English language learners in their classes.

## FINDING SOLUTIONS THAT WORK

Just as school programs of the past have given way to more innovative and effective approaches for English language learners, so too have the strategies used to teach content. In fact, today's teachers familiar with past practices in content classrooms might even be reluctant to use the term *strategy* to describe them.

### Past Attempts

Past attempts to teach content to students who lacked well-developed English language skills were generally pedagogically inadequate and affectively harsh.

Perhaps the most widespread approach was simply to ignore these students. Content learning was put on hold while they were in the process of learning English. After all, how could they possibly be expected to learn content when they didn't even know the English language!

Other teachers erred in the opposite direction. Instead of ignoring the students themselves, they ignored the fact that these students' *needs* were different. The students were required to do the same work as the rest of the class. The inevitable result of this approach was a year or more of students facing high stress, failing grades, and low self-esteem.

Some schools took more active measures to deal with the situation. Recognizing that a student who didn't know any English should not be expected to perform successfully in an on-grade classroom, these schools placed these new students in considerably lower grade levels. This was, again, hardly an adaptive solution.

Even teachers who empathized with the plight of these students didn't have much to offer them. To involve them in classroom activities, these teachers devised busywork assignments to fill the class period. Students were kept occupied by drawing or coloring content-related pictures and by doing classroom housekeeping chores. Although decidedly less stressful, this approach was again unproductive.

Low expectations and lack of understanding underlay all of these practices. The common belief was that students needed to wait until they learned English before they could begin to learn content. Fortunately, the experiences of creative teachers using innovative approaches clearly demonstrate that this does not have to be the case.

## A Better Way: Scaffolding

Teachers, facing ever-increasing numbers of English language learners in today's classrooms, are now using solutions that work. More effective approaches involving adaptive strategies for textbooks, assignments, instruction, and assessment have been developed so that English language learners *can* learn content *while* they are learning English. These approaches are widely referred to as *ESOL strategies*. A newer term is *scaffolded instruction* or just *scaffolding*.

ESOL is the acronym for *English for Speakers of Other Languages*. It is one of several commonly used terms to refer to programs for English language learners and the students themselves. (Other terms are listed in the Glossary of Acronyms in Appendix I at the end of this book.) Despite the fact that the term *ESOL* has gained a negative connotation in some areas, it continues to be the most widely used and recognized term. *ESOL strategies*, then, refer to the many techniques that are used to modify classroom practices to make content more comprehensible for ESOL students.

The term *scaffolding* came into usage because it so well described the way ESOL strategies were designed to work. Language learners use ESOL strategies in the same way that construction workers use scaffolds in the process of building. In construction, scaffolds are temporary external structures that provide the supports upon which workers stand as they construct a building. They allow access to parts of the construction that would be otherwise impossible to reach. When the work is completed, the scaffolds come down. So, too, it is with scaffolded instruction.

Scaffolding, or using ESOL strategies, provides students with the support they need to learn content while they are building their English language skills. In ways figuratively similar to construction, academic scaffolds help language learners access content. The scaffolds will be progressively dismantled and discarded as they are no longer useful.

## THE REWARDS OF SCAFFOLDED INSTRUCTION

Using ESOL strategies to scaffold your instruction will enable English language learners to learn better by increasing their level of interest and motivation in the content you teach. Human nature is such that most people show little interest in things they can't or don't understand. Even if initially interested, most learners react to not "getting it" by simply turning off and tuning out. Feelings of interest quickly give way to feelings of frustration.

Unfortunately, it is precisely that interest—the perceived need or desire to learn—that forms one of the most powerful motivators to learning. Individuals pay more attention and learn faster when they really *want* to learn something. Learning is easier, quicker, and more readily retained when it is motivated by interest.

Using ESOL strategies to scaffold instruction prevents feelings of frustration from overwhelming English language learners' interest and desire to learn. English language learners become more interested in content because they are able to understand it better. The more motivated they are to learn, the more they actually do learn.

Scaffolding instruction also helps students develop feelings of self-confidence. As English language learners begin to experience success in learning content, they begin to get an "I can do this" feeling. They develop confidence in themselves as learners. The more they believe in themselves as learners, the better learners they actually become. One success leads to many others and they grow as learners, both in content knowledge and in English language ability. The old adage, *nothing succeeds like success*, holds much truth.

An indirect benefit of scaffolded instruction lies in the area of the students' cultural and social adjustment. Many students entering U.S. schools from other countries have come from successful academic environments. Schooling for these students has been a source of satisfaction and achievement, both socially and academically. These are the same students who now find themselves in a school environment that fills them with feelings of frustration and isolation.

The teacher who facilitates comprehension for these students by using ESOL strategies is helping to reestablish school as a place of positive rewards. It is an important contribution to these students' adjustment to life in a new country.

Scaffolding offers rewards for teachers as well. You derive satisfaction from knowing that you've connected with the English language learners in your classroom and that you've engaged them in the learning process. In fact, you may discover that scaffolding instruction has an even wider effect—some of your *native* English-speaking students may benefit from the additional support as well. Scaffolding can make them feel more successful, too. Both you and your students derive greater satisfaction from your teaching. You view yourself with renewed confidence. You are an accomplished professional.

## A FINAL THOUGHT

You chose to become a math, science, or social studies teacher because the subject matter was exciting to you. You clearly did *not* choose this field because you hoped to focus on teaching language skills. But without a brief acquaintance with those language skills, your English language learners are unable to access the content you teach. Scaffolded instruction helps bridge that gap.

ESOL strategies offer you options—strategies, techniques, ideas, and activities—to help you make better instructional decisions. They are the keys that will unlock new doorways to student knowledge and achievement. Dramatic? Yes, but you will actually see that you've made a real difference in the lives and learning of these students.

# CHAPTER 2

# Language, Learning, and Content Instruction

## WHAT DO YOU KNOW WHEN YOU KNOW A LANGUAGE?

Have you ever thought about what you know when you know a language? Most people's first reaction is to say, "You know how to speak, read, and write it." But you also know a great deal more. You know vocabulary and grammar. You know how to put words together so that someone will understand what you're trying to say. You know how to choose the right words and phrases to deal appropriately with a wide variety of circumstances and people. You know the idioms, the proverbs, and the common cultural references of the language.

You understand intended meaning based on intonation. The messages of single words like *really*, *oh*, and *interesting* change entirely depending on how they are voiced. Few native speakers would confuse the meaning of "Really?" with "Really!"

You know the order to place adjectives that modify a noun. You would never say anything like "the brick big red house." You recognize that certain words go together because of common usage. You say *heavy smoker* but *weighty matter*—and never *weighty smoker* or *heavy matter* (unless, of course, you're talking science).

You understand the subtle differences in meaning behind very close synonyms. Your choice of describing an acquaintance's appearance as *slim*, *thin*, or *skinny* or someone's behavior as *childlike* instead of *childish* has everything to do with your feelings of approval or disapproval.

You understand that certain words are group nouns and can't be individually counted. You say *three suitcases* but never *three luggages*. You know that prepositions can change the meaning of a phrase. You wouldn't confuse a sign that said *On Sale* with one that said *For Sale*.

Amazing, isn't it? You, as a fluent speaker of English, possess an enormous amount of language knowledge. That's because you learned English either as your first language or early in your childhood. Because you were immersed in an English language environment, you acquired oral language skills naturally and easily, and probably have not given much thought to the subtleties of vocabulary and grammar.

Your years of schooling developed your written language skills and added polish to your oral skills. Your teacher training years focused on acquiring knowledge of the content you teach and methods to effectively teach it. Unlike teachers of English whose subject matter is the English language itself, your expertise lies in your knowledge of the math, science, or social studies you teach. Yet without the same preparation and depth of understanding about language and language acquisition as those teachers of English, you are expected to make your content comprehensible to the English language learners in your classes. To help you reach them and teach them, there are a few basic concepts about language that are important for you to know.

## LANGUAGE AS A SOCIAL SKILL

Language is a social construct; the purpose of language is communication. Adult speakers of other languages who move to the United States first learn English to satisfy their basic needs. They often attend English language classes that teach "survival skills," such as asking questions and reading newspaper want ads so that they can find their way around the neighborhood, rent an apartment, apply for a job, and register their children in school.

Children's basic needs are less complex. Children need to make friends with other children. They need to communicate while they play together. They need to participate in the youth culture of sports, games, music, TV, videogames, movies, fads, and fashion. Young children whose native language is not English develop the language skills for these activities by becoming immersed in an English language–rich environment—school. There, for about six hours a day, they receive constant language input through which they learn the language to fulfill these needs and interests. It is a process of natural acquisition rather than any type of formal instruction. It bears many similarities to the process of first language development in young children.

The skills these English language learners are developing are called *Basic Interpersonal Communicative Skills*, or *BICS* for short. BICS is the language of everyday activities: the way we communicate with others in a social environment. Children learning English develop BICS with an apparent ease that often awes adult learners. In fact, in children, competent BICS takes only from six months to three years to acquire.

## LANGUAGE AS AN ACADEMIC SKILL

Schools have traditionally judged the proficiency level of English language learners by assessing their oral language skills. This, however, can be a highly misleading indicator. The language that children need to succeed in school is quite different from the oral language they use in social contexts. Even students who function at a high level in face-to-face social interaction may lack critical language skills for learning academic content. You may find yourself puzzled at this point. Don't you speak the same English inside your classroom as you do outside of it? The answer to that question is both *yes* and *no*.

On a surface level, it *is* the same. But what teachers ask students to do with language inside the classroom is much more complex than what students do with language outside in the real world. School is a place of high expectations and academic challenge. In the environment of the classroom, students are asked to engage in academic thinking skills that involve problem solving and critical thinking. Every dimension of learning requires students to demonstrate proficiency in using cognitive language skills. In a typical school day, students will use language to

- Participate in small group or whole class oral discussions about issues and ideas
- Give oral responses to the teacher's questions
- Listen to learn content from the teacher's spoken words (lower grades)
- Simultaneously listen, take notes, and process content (higher grades)
- Observe, interpret, and process science experiments, graphs, maps, videos, and other visual aids
- Read to gather information and build knowledge
- Write to complete homework assignments, projects, reports, and research

These classroom language skills are quite different from those used in social contexts. Social language, or BICS, involves such abilities as retelling events, describing experiences, narrating activities, offering personal opinions, all within the general give-and-take of conversation with family and friends.

The language of the classroom makes conceptual demands on language that are beyond the scope of BICS talk. In the classroom, students are asked to do things with language that are more abstract and cognitively complex. Academic assignments require students to use language to

| | |
|---|---|
| compare | explain |
| contrast | analyze |
| list | discuss |
| define | infer |
| order | justify |
| classify | integrate |
| describe | evaluate |
| predict | deduce |

Students must perform these functions in all the modalities of language—speaking, listening, reading, and writing. These classroom language skills are collectively known as *cognitive academic language proficiency*, or *CALP*.

## UNDERSTANDING CALP

CALP and BICS, then, use language for different purposes. CALP is used in a classroom environment and deals with theory and concepts. BICS is used in a social environment and deals with the here-and-now of everyday life. The language of CALP is generally cognitively challenging (i.e., hard), while the language of BICS is generally cognitively unchallenging (i.e., easy).

There is a second factor that affects the difficulty of language for English language learners. Spoken and written language is difficult in isolation—that is, without any environmental clues to meaning. Words become clearer when they are surrounded or embedded in a background environment that serves to assist comprehension.

Cummins,[1] who contributed the concept of BICS and CALP, created a graphic (Figure 2.1) to aid in understanding what makes language easier or harder for English language learners. Difficulty is based on the relationship between the two factors: the cognitive demand of the task and the amount of available contextual support.

The first factor, the degree of cognitive challenge, is represented in Cummins's framework as basically easy or hard. The two quadrants across the top of Cummins's chart represent oral or written tasks that are cognitively undemanding—either largely social or simply academically easy. The two lower quadrants of the chart represent tasks that are cognitively demanding. These tasks are academically difficult, requiring higher levels of thought processing and language skills.

The second factor in Cummins's framework evaluates the amount of contextual support inherent in the task. Contextual supports offer clues to the meaning of words. The more spoken and written words are supported or embedded in context, the easier they are to understand. Spoken language can be given contextual support through facial expressions, gestures, body language, demonstrations, and visual cues from the physical environment. Written language can offer contextual support through pictures, graphs, charts, tables, and textbook aids. Oral and written tasks with these kinds of supports are called *context-embedded*. Tasks in which students have only the spoken or written words alone to work with are termed *context-reduced*.

The two quadrants on the left side of Cummins's chart represent tasks that are highly embedded and contextually supported. Tasks in the two quadrants

---

[1]Cummins, J. *Bilingualism and Special Education: Issues in Assessment and Pedagogy.* (San Francisco, CA: College-Hill Press, 1984).

| I<br><br>Cognitively<br><br>Undemanding<br><br>+<br><br>Context-embedded | II<br><br>Cognitively<br><br>Undemanding<br><br>+<br><br>Context-reduced |
|---|---|
| III<br><br>Cognitively<br><br>Demanding<br><br>+<br><br>Context-embedded | IV<br><br>Cognitively<br><br>Demanding<br><br>+<br><br>Context-reduced |

**FIGURE 2.1. Cummins's Framework for Evaluating Language Demand in Content Activities (Modified Format)**

on the right side are context-reduced. Combining the two elements of cognitive challenge and contextual support, the quadrants move in difficulty from I to IV. English language learners will generally find Quadrant I tasks easy because they are low in cognitive demand and high in contextual support. Quadrant IV tasks are at the other extreme; these tasks will be difficult for ELLs because they are academically demanding and lack contextual support.

Actual examples of tasks in each of the four quadrants, as shown in Figure 2.2, will help clarify Cummins's chart. Face-to-face conversations fall into Quadrant I. The task of making conversation is social and therefore not particularly cognitively demanding. Contextual support for spoken words comes from watching the speaker's lips and observing facial expressions and body language. The task moves to Quadrant II when the same conversation takes place over the telephone. While the task is still social, the listener loses the speaker's contextual support and must rely completely on auditory input for comprehension.

The tasks illustrating Quadrants III and IV are similar. On the lower half of the chart, the tasks are cognitively challenging. English language learners (and other students as well) will find mathematical word problems that offer the contextual support of manipulatives, graphics, and/or pictures easier to solve than problems without these aids. Again, the difficulty is affected by how well the words are embedded in context.

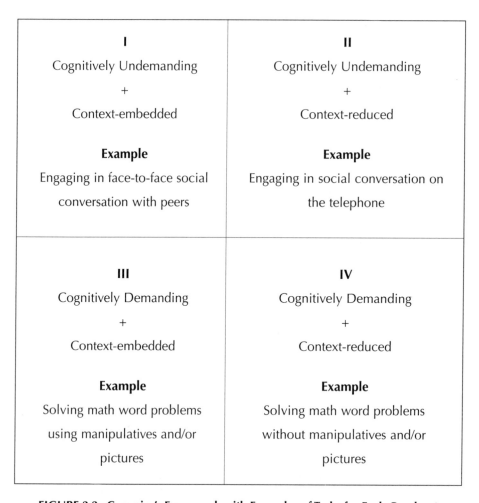

| I | II |
|---|---|
| Cognitively Undemanding | Cognitively Undemanding |
| + | + |
| Context-embedded | Context-reduced |
| **Example** | **Example** |
| Engaging in face-to-face social conversation with peers | Engaging in social conversation on the telephone |
| III | IV |
| Cognitively Demanding | Cognitively Demanding |
| + | + |
| Context-embedded | Context-reduced |
| **Example** | **Example** |
| Solving math word problems using manipulatives and/or pictures | Solving math word problems without manipulatives and/or pictures |

**FIGURE 2.2. Cummins's Framework with Examples of Tasks for Each Quadrant**

Here is a list of additional examples of tasks in each of the quadrants. Can you figure out why each one is assigned to its particular quadrant?

*Quadrant I*

- Engaging in social conversation with peers
- Ordering dinner from a picture menu in a fast food restaurant
- Listening to a presentation about pet animals that includes pictures and video
- Participating in physical education classes

### Quadrant II

- Getting information via the telephone
- Ordering dinner from a menu in a formal restaurant
- Listening to an audio presentation about caring for pets
- Reading a list of required school supplies

### Quadrant III

- Solving simple math computation problems
- Solving math word problems using manipulatives and/or pictures
- Doing a science experiment by following a demonstration
- Understanding written text through pictures, graphics, and small group discussion
- Reading the illustrated (comic book) version of Shakespeare's *Romeo and Juliet*

### Quadrant IV

- Solving math word problems without manipulatives and/or pictures
- Doing a science experiment by reading directions from a textbook
- Writing research reports on assigned topics in social studies
- Listening to a lecture on an unfamiliar topic
- Reading Shakespeare's *Romeo and Juliet* in its original format

Not every task can be neatly placed in a quadrant. Variables within a task itself or within a student's prior knowledge or experience can affect its placement on the chart. For example, the task of solving simple math computational problems listed under Quadrant III would have to be moved to Quadrant IV if a student's native language used a different system of notation for writing numerals.

An even more complex example is the Quadrant I entry, participating in physical education classes. Where this task is placed depends entirely on what is involved. It would remain a Quadrant I task if it involved *demonstrating* how to play a game or sport. It would become a Quadrant II task if the rules of play were only orally explained. It would move into the cognitively demanding quadrants if it involved discussions and/or readings about complex rules and regulations of play or about the history of a sport. Placing these tasks in either Quadrant III or Quadrant IV would depend upon the amount of available contextual support. Similarly, participation in physical education classes might also fall into Quadrant III or IV when they include learning about health and hygiene issues.

Tasks assigned as classwork and homework are typically cognitively demanding and often context-reduced (Quadrant IV). For students to experience success with this type of schoolwork, their academic language skills, CALP, must be at or near grade level. English language learners haven't yet reached that level. Even ELLs with good academic language skills in their native language are still in the process of developing this proficiency in English. The more familiar content teachers are with the concept of CALP and how it develops, the better able they will be to help the English language learners in their classrooms. They will be able to select, plan, and use appropriate strategies that move content learning from Quadrant IV to Quadrant III.

## LANGUAGE AND CONTENT TEACHING

Academic language skills are complex, cognitively demanding, and situation-specific. They take from five to seven years to reach full development because they are specific to the academic world. Unlike BICS, which are learned naturally from the environment, CALP is learned only in the classroom in a process that is long and complicated. Indeed, developing and refining the skills of CALP is one of the objectives underlying the elementary school curriculum.

### How CALP Develops

The elementary school years can be viewed as a six-year course in developing academic language and thinking skills. In the primary grades, students learn the basic skills of language. Along with early reading and writing skills, they also begin to learn how to listen, how to observe, and how to think academically. Content learning in the primary grades is taught largely through visual, manipulative, and experiential means. Instruction is facilitated and context-embedded for all students.

English language learners and native speakers alike are going through a similar process of learning: They all enter kindergarten needing to learn the most basic academic skills of language. The primary grades of elementary school focus large blocks of time on developing the skills involved in reading and writing for all students, regardless of their language background.

The intermediate grades of elementary school involve students in language instruction that promotes higher levels of conceptual development and communicative ability. There is a shift in focus from *learning to read* to *reading to learn*. Students are now regularly required to think, talk, read, and write about content. They are given assignments that require them to engage in critical reading and literary criticism (also known as book reports); observations and write-ups of science experiments; research and reports on geography, economics, and culture in social studies; and complex calculations and word problems in math.

These experiences in the elementary school years constitute the foundation of academic language learning. Students are expected to build upon this foundation as they move through middle school and high school. Their academic language ability becomes the medium through which they must demonstrate the attainment of specific content knowledge at higher and higher levels each year in their classes.

So how do English language learners entering U.S. schools fit into this plan? Those entering in the primary grade years have the easiest task for two reasons. First, for young children, school presents a natural language learning environment. Their BICS develop through daily immersion in the language-rich activities of the classroom. They acquire the oral skills of language in a seemingly effortless manner. The second factor easing the way for young ELLs is that primary grade content instruction is context-embedded for *all* students. Language skills development is just beginning. Because academic reading, writing, listening, and thinking skills are at such an early stage of development, all approaches to content learning must rely heavily on contextual supports.

The situation changes dramatically after the primary school years. By third grade, students are expected to have achieved a minimum level of academic language proficiency. This is the year of the shift: Third graders, while still learning to read, are now beginning to *use* their reading skills to learn.

English language learners entering the American school system face challenges to learning content that grow with each school year. Starting in third or fourth grade and increasing year by year through high school, expectations of knowledge and achievement for all students rise to successively higher levels. Students who must learn academic English language skills at the same time that they are expected to acquire content knowledge face a dauntingly demanding situation.

Teachers of math, science, social studies, and other content areas can ease the path for English language learners by utilizing strategies that will contextualize the content they teach—in other words, by moving instruction from Quadrant IV to Quadrant III. These strategies offer options and ideas to make better decisions about content teaching and assessment. They are the focus of Parts II and III of this book.

# CHAPTER 3

# Culture, Learning, and Content Instruction

---

**Case Study—Return to Mr. Elkind's Classroom**

Mr. Elkind, the social studies teacher, has excellent rapport with his students. Several times during the school year, he seeks students' input about the methods, materials, assignments, and projects he uses to teach. Students can sign their names or not, as they wish. Their feedback is generally positive. From what the students say, Mr. Elkind believes that they like his teaching style and the types of interaction and activities in his classroom. That's the feedback from his native English-speaking students; from his English language learners, it's a different story. Most of them don't answer the questions at all, and he's sure it's *not* because they can't read or understand them. He empathizes with their position and the challenges they face, but sometimes he's just plain baffled by some of the things they do—or don't do. It feels like a puzzle to him, and he'd like to solve it.

---

## CULTURE AND LEARNING

The solution to at least one large piece of Mr. Elkind's puzzle can be stated in a single word: *culture*. Culture may be defined as the shared beliefs and values that determine the rule-governed patterns of behavior of individuals within the cultural group. Culture is made up of many parts: values, beliefs, standards of beauty, patterns of thinking, norms of behavior, styles of communication. Among other things, culture determines how its group members interact with others. Culture goes beyond the sum of its parts; it is the eyes through which individuals view the world.

English language learners in U.S. schools are not only learning a new language, but also a new culture—the culture of American schools. There exists the potential for cross-cultural misunderstandings between teacher and ELL student.

Because culture shapes group members' ideas of politeness and etiquette, students from other cultures often react in class in ways that vary beyond the range of American cultural norms. Students from outside the United States carry their culture with them and respond with behaviors that are considered appropriate and polite within their own group. Teachers who do not realize the cultural context of these responses often mistakenly interpret them as individual rudeness, disinterest, or lack of knowledge. Developing an awareness of culture as a determinant of a foreign student's response will help teachers to depersonalize these behaviors and view them on a cultural level. The next sections will examine a number of the frequently misunderstood areas of communication.

## Classwork Patterns

The typical classroom uses whole class, small group, and individual work formats. In American schools, effective instruction consists of balancing the three types. In cultures that place more value on group cooperation, however, misunderstandings of intent can occur when individual work is required, as in a testing situation. Other cultures, in contrast, view the teacher as the academic authority and therefore the only appropriate source of learning. Students from this type of educational background may view group work as nonproductive and may be reluctant to participate in it.

## Instructional Formats

Critical thinking, problem solving, and discovery learning are the gold standards of American instructional approaches. School programs in foreign countries, on the other hand, may put greater emphasis on techniques of rote memorization for learning. Students from these cultures may experience difficulty in understanding the instructional process. The true story described in Figure 3.1 on page 20 is an example of this type of misunderstanding.

## Questioning Patterns

American classrooms value students who ask questions, seek clarification, and challenge statements and ideas. Many cultures, however, do not encourage expressing personal opinions or questioning the teacher in class.

Students from some cultures may not be willing to participate in discussions that involve expressing opposing opinions or beliefs. For students whose culture teaches them that it is rude and disrespectful to disagree with an authority figure, offering an opinion that differs from that of the teacher is simply not an option. Even disagreeing with peers may seem impolite to students with this background.

Yasmin's English skills were actually quite good, but she rarely participated in class. About halfway through the first semester, Ms. Dennis, her teacher, had a conference with her to talk about her lack of participation. Yasmin had a ready answer. She explained that each night, she read and memorized all the information in the textbook. But the next day in class, the teacher asked "other" questions—not questions about the facts in the book.

It was a "lightbulb moment" for Ms. Dennis. Yasmin was 100% correct in her assessment of the situation. Ms. Dennis viewed the information in the textbook as a knowledge base and used class time to build upon that knowledge. Her questions guided students to extend their conceptual understandings by engaging them in critical thinking and problem-solving tasks. Yasmin's prior academic experience had not prepared her for this approach to instruction.

**FIGURE 3.1. True Tale: Cross-Cultural Misunderstanding**

Asking questions and seeking clarification may also be viewed in unexpected ways. Some students may feel it will cause the teacher embarrassment since not understanding reflects poorly on the teacher's knowledge and ability to teach. Other students may view questions as rude interruptions. Teachers who invite this type of interaction may be seen as lacking control and authority in their classrooms.

Teachers often lead discussions by asking questions and calling on students who raise their hands. Cultural beliefs, however, may prevent some students from volunteering answers. Students from cultures that deeply value humility may never raise their hands because displaying knowledge is considered a form of showing off.

In many cultures, adults are viewed as the figures of authority, and children are taught not to speak until they are spoken to. These students are following their cultural values by not volunteering information, not questioning for clarification, and not seeking additional information. On the other hand, calling on a student who doesn't volunteer may produce an unintended effect if the student is from a culture in which wrong answers are felt to bring shame on oneself and one's family.

## Response Time

Americans, in general, value conversation and are uncomfortable with silence. Those who follow the rules of conversation—rules for when to speak, how and when to interrupt, and how many people can speak at the same time—are thought to be polite. Interestingly, these rules vary not only across cultures, but also regionally across the United States.

Americans, in general, become anxious with conversational silences lasting longer than several seconds. Some cultures, however, are comfortable with much longer periods of silence. Children from these cultures learn that it is a sign of courtesy, respect, and wisdom to take time before responding. Other cultures, in contrast, value responses that are loud and quick. Those who jump right in to answer are seen as interested, involved, and even strong.

These variations in culturally appropriate response patterns may cause teachers to misinterpret student behaviors during class discussions. Teachers may characterize students who don't immediately reply to questions as slow or lacking knowledge, and to those who jump right in as rude, domineering, or overanxious. Teachers who can depersonalize these behaviors by repositioning them in a cultural context will be able to see these students in a more positive light and help them adjust to more appropriate classroom behaviors.

## Attention Patterns

Americans like eye contact—it shows that the listener is paying attention. Most teachers like to see every student looking directly at them while they teach. When students nod their heads as well, teachers feel well understood and enthusiastically appreciated. Although teachers may view lack of eye contact as a sign of disrespect or disinterest, other cultures view these behaviors differently. Downcast eyes in some cultures show respect for the speaker, especially when the speaker is a figure of authority. Direct eye contact with an adult, especially a teacher, is considered overt boldness or defiant behavior.

Head nods, in many cultures, do not signify agreement or indicate understanding. Head nods simply show that the speaker is being heard. Additionally, some cultures place great value on emotional control and discourage any show of enthusiasm or confirmation through changes in facial features.

## Feedback Patterns

Americans are generally effusive in their use of praise. Teachers are generous in doling out intrinsic and extrinsic rewards as reinforcement for notable achievement and good behavior. They use praise to encourage students to continue their efforts to learn. Positive reinforcement theory recommends finding even small successes to praise.

In contrast, certain cultures believe that praise should be reserved only for true excellence and outstanding performance. Praise given too frequently or too generously is seen as insincere. Teachers who praise too much may even be viewed as inadequate—if students are so praiseworthy, perhaps the teacher just doesn't know all that much more than the students. Alternatively, praise offered in front of the whole class may bring feelings of shame to students whose culture values humility.

Misunderstandings can also occur in the area of error correction. Some cultures strive for academic perfection to a greater degree than U.S. school culture does. To those students, a teacher's lack of constant correction may be viewed, like too much praise, as a sign of inadequacy.

Written feedback may also cause misunderstanding. Not all countries use the common notations of ✓ for right and X for wrong. It is possible that they, too, may be subject to misinterpretation.

## A SHIFT IN PERCEPTION

An awareness of areas of potential cross-cultural misunderstanding will allow teachers to see their ELL students in a clearer light. Reactively, thinking *culture* as the source of a student's behavior will help to refocus the way you perceive what is happening in your classroom. Proactively, some of the things you can do to ease cultural adjustment issues for ELLs include:

- Varying classwork formats and explaining the purpose of each type
- Praising something specific in a student's response rather than repeating the generic "Very good"
- Modeling and discussing appropriate classroom behaviors such as asking and answering questions, offering an opinion or point of view, and taking turns
- Allowing extended wait time to students whose culture values it
- Explaining the meaning of your written correction symbols
- Learning about other cultures by talking to adults familiar with those cultures or by doing Internet research

### Cultural Beliefs Change Slowly

A change in culturally ingrained behavior may take some time. Students who become familiar with the variations in cultural expectations will probably not be able to put those behaviors into immediate effect. Understanding that American students who volunteer answers, for example, are not showing off will not make ELLs want to behave in that manner themselves. Their feelings about that type of behavior will lag behind their rational understanding of it. The roots of culture are very deep.

## THE CULTURE OF CONTENT

A few words about content-specific issues will complete this cursory look at culture in the classroom. While certain issues like the notation of dates and time shown in Figure 3.2 cross all content areas, there are a number of particular cross-cultural matters that teachers of math, science, and social studies each have to consider when teaching their subjects to English language learners.

| U.S. Notation | Foreign Notation |
|---|---|
| **Dates** | |
| month/day/year | day/month/year |
| 7/22/04 | 22/7/04 |
| **Time** | |
| 12-hour clock with colon + a.m./ p.m. | 24-hour clock with period |
| hour:minute | hour.minute |
| 8:40 a.m. | 08.40 |
| 1:30 p.m. | 13.30 |
| 8:40 p.m. | 20.40 |

**FIGURE 3.2.  Differences in Writing Dates and Times**

## Special Considerations for Teachers of Math

Starting at the most basic level, students from foreign countries may form the numerals differently from American notation. Figure 3.3 shows the numerals as a typical European-schooled student would write them. Additionally, some areas teach writing the 0 with a line through it, so it looks like this: Ø

**FIGURE 3.3.  European Notation of Numerals**

Numbers are highly ingrained in students' native language. Counting in English is particularly difficult, even for those with well-developed English language skills. The fact that fully bilingual speakers can test which language is their dominant one by mentally observing which language they count in illustrates how deeply rooted numbers and counting really are. Reading large numbers correctly and understanding large numbers orally are skills that improve slowly with a great deal of practice.

Mathematical usage of decimal points and commas in written notation is another area of potential confusion. Many foreign countries use a system that is opposite from U.S. notation. Periods replace commas to mark off hundreds in large numbers, and commas are used in place of periods to mark off decimal places, as shown in Figure 3.4. Additionally, in some countries, the meaning of *billion* varies from the U.S. concept of billion as one thousand million. In those places, one billion is equal to one million million.

| | U.S. Notation | Foreign Notation |
|---|---|---|
| Grouping Hundreds | 7,234,567 | 7.234.567 |
| Marking Decimal Places | 98.6 | 98,6 |
| Showing Prices | $12.89 | €12,89 (Euro) |
| | | £12,89 (Pounds Sterling) |

FIGURE 3.4. Opposite Usage of Commas and Periods in Numeric Notation

Most of the world's countries use the metric system to measure weight, volume, and distance. Foreign students will be accustomed to calculating measurements in meters, liters, kilograms, and kilometers. They again need practice to learn and become comfortable with the U.S. system of feet, quarts, pounds, and miles.

Another area of possible cultural difference is in the focus on process so prevalent in American schools. Some cultures focus more on computational skills. For students coming from those cultures, the final answer is more valued than the process of finding the answer. The teacher's request to "show your work" may be difficult to honor since grades would have been penalized for doing so in their native country.

Schools in foreign countries may also teach different algorithms for computation. Figures 3.5 through 3.7 illustrate several unusual techniques for computation. If students in your classes are accustomed to using these

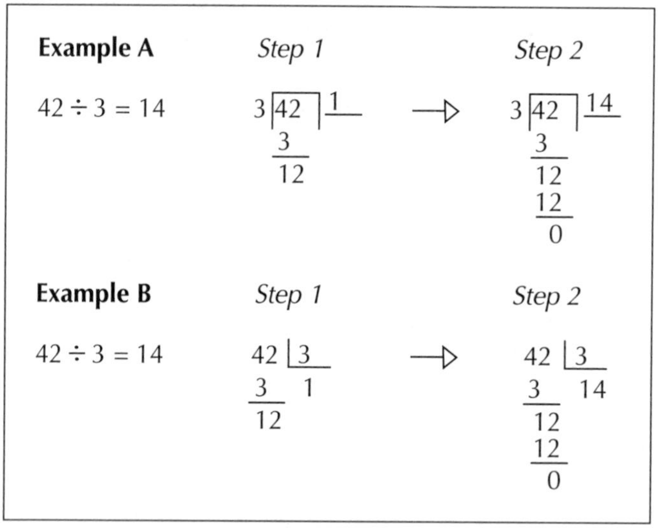

FIGURE 3.5. Alternate Styles of Division

**Example**                                    *Computation*

$32 \times 16 = 512$                                    32
                                                    $\times\,16$
                                                    192
                                                     32
                                                    512

*Check*

**1.** Draw a large $\times$.

**2.** Add the digits of the first number (32) together: $3 + 2 = 5$.

    Place the sum in the *top* section.

**3.** Add the digits of the second number (16) together: $1 + 6 = 7$.

    Place the sum in the *bottom* section.

**4.** Multiply the two numbers now in the $\times$:

    $5 \times 7 = 35$.

    Add the two digits together: $3 + 5 = 8$.

    Place the sum in the *left* section.

**5.** Add all digits in the products (512) together:

    $5 + 1 + 2 = 8$.

    Place the sum in the *right* section.

If the LEFT and the RIGHT sections are the same, the product is correct.

**FIGURE 3.6. An Unusual Technique to Check Multiplication Problems**

approaches, it is best to let them continue the practice. Ask students to demonstrate how they arrive at an answer. You and your students will be fascinated, and your English language learners may, in the process, earn some extra esteem and respect.

**Example**          *Computation*

$89 \times 47 = 4183$

$$
\begin{array}{r}
89 \\
\times\, 47 \\
\hline
623 \\
356\phantom{0} \\
\hline
4183
\end{array}
$$

*Note:* Only a single digit can be placed in the four sections of the $\times$. When the sum of any set of digits is more than a single digit, as in this example, add the second sum of digits together *again* to produce a single digit.

*Check*

1. Add the digits of the first number (89) together: $8 + 9 = 17$.

    Add the digits (17) together again: $1 + 7 = 8$.

    Place the sum in the *top* section.

2. Add the digits of the second number (47) together: $4 + 7 = 11$.

    Add the digits (11) together again: $1 + 1 = 2$.

    Place the sum in the *bottom* section.

3. Multiply the two numbers now in the $\times$: $8 \times 2 = 16$.

    Add the two digits together: $1 + 6 = 7$.

    Place the sum in the *left* section.

4. Add all digits in the products (4183) together:

    $4 + 1 + 8 + 3 = 16$.

    Add the digits (16) together again: $1 + 6 = 7$.

    Place the sum in the *right* section.

If the LEFT and the RIGHT sections are the same, the product is correct. It ALWAYS works!

**FIGURE 3.7. It always works—here is another example**

## Special Considerations for Teachers of Science

Teachers of science should be aware that for students from other parts of the world, science might not be as "pure" as Americans tend to think. Cultural backgrounds and religious teachings are strong determinants of beliefs. Students from other countries may hold conflicting views of commonly accepted scientific beliefs. Additionally, there may be strong cultural taboos that affect the study of science. Activities such as dissecting animals and handling human bones, for example, may be forbidden.

Like math teachers, teachers of science are unquestionably aware of the difference between U.S. measurement systems and those used in most other countries. Students from countries using the metric system will be unfamiliar with our measurements of ounces, pounds, tons, cups, pints, quarts, gallons, inches, feet, yards, and miles. In terms of heat measurements, the Centigrade scale is more widely used than Fahrenheit. It will take some practice for students to feel comfortable using U.S. measurement systems.

## Special Considerations for Teachers of Social Studies

Social studies is a nationalistic subject: Students everywhere learn about the people, places, and events that comprise the tapestry of world history from a nation-centered standpoint. The view is global, but the focus is local. Wars, conquests, alliances, power shifts, and leaders are subject to local interpretation. Inhabitants of neighboring countries as well as those considerably more distanced may see the same historical events in a very different light. The particular understanding of history that English language learners are familiar with may differ from the one U.S.-schooled students have learned.

Additionally, in many parts of the world, history is rewritten as new rulers come into power. Current national, regional, ethnic, and religious perspectives color the way the past is seen. George Orwell, in his novel *1984*, wrote, "Who controls the past controls the future: Who controls the present controls the past." It is important that teachers recognize these potential disparities.

As a final note to this chapter, it is worth repeating that human beings are products of their culture. Culture and cultural beliefs are deeply ingrained; they are not easily changed or discarded. Teachers of all subjects need to develop an awareness of cultural determinants of behavior and a sensitivity to possible cultural conflicts to learning.

# PART II

# Strategies for Instruction

# CHAPTER 4

# Learning Strategies: An Overview Focusing on English Language Learners

**Case Study—Rosalia**

Rosalia looks at the assigned word problems in her math book and knows that there is no way she can possibly figure out any of the answers. It's not that Rosalia's math skills are weak. In fact, she knows she's really pretty good at computation. She also knows that, once again, it's all those words in the problem that will bar her way to success. Rosalia is an English language learner.

For Rosalia, perhaps even more than the native English-speakers in her classes, learning strategies are the keys to academic success. Successful learners in all subject areas are ones who have discovered and developed techniques of learning that work best for them. They have available to them a repertoire of learning strategies and know which to select to meet their immediate learning needs. They have acquired the tools of successful academic learning.

All students need to use learning strategies, and all students benefit from direct instruction in how to use them. English language learners, even more so, need this guidance to overcome the challenge of learning a new language while trying to use that language to learn content.

## LEARNING STRATEGIES: A SIMPLE DEFINITION

Learning strategies are techniques that facilitate the process of understanding, retaining, and applying knowledge. They are the "tricks of the learning trade." They come in many varieties, but not all strategies work equally well for all learners. Exposure to different types allows students to develop their own personal menu of strategies—a repertoire of strategies that work well for them. They choose appropriate strategies to fit the type of knowledge they need to learn in combination with their personal learning styles. For ELLs in content classrooms, these tricks of the learning trade take on extra importance and value.

## TYPES OF LEARNING STRATEGIES

There are a number of ways to classify learning strategies. Many systems recognize three types: metacognitive, cognitive, and social. English language learners benefit from the addition of two more: memory strategies, a specialized subtype of the cognitive strategy type, and compensation strategies. It is important to understand how each of these types helps students learn.

**Metacognitive** strategies are those that involve *thinking* about learning. These can be divided into two subtypes of techniques: those that deal with *organizing* and *planning* for learning, and those that deal with *self-monitoring* and *self-evaluating* learning.

### Examples of Metacognitive Strategies Dealing with Organizing and Planning for Learning

- Using a homework notebook to write down all assignments
- Keeping a calendar/organizer to write down long-term assignments
- Dividing long-term assignments into shorter segments and tasks
- Setting deadlines for completion of each segment or task
- Determining the most appropriate and efficient strategies to learn specific content
- Planning *how* to study for a test

### Examples of Metacognitive Strategies Dealing with Self-monitoring and Self-evaluating Learning

- Recognizing your own knowledge gaps or weaknesses
- Discovering strategies that work best for you (and those that don't)
- Checking up on yourself by frequently responding to the little voice inside your head that asks, *"How am I doing?"*

**Cognitive** strategies are those that involve any type of *practice* activity. They are techniques that promote deeper understanding, better retention, and/or increased ability to apply new knowledge. The techniques that fall into this category are familiar to successful learners and are used on a regular basis.

### Examples of Cognitive Strategies

- Making specific connections between new learning and old
- Making connections between English and the student's native language
- Highlighting important information while reading
- Dividing a large body of information into smaller units
- Note taking (even in student's native language)
- Condensing notes to study for a test
- Making and using flash cards to test yourself
- Making visual associations to aid in retention
- Creating graphic organizers, maps, charts, diagrams, time lines, and flow charts to organize information
- Making categories and classifications

Cognitive strategies form the core of learning techniques. They fall into the general category that students call "studying." Cognitive strategies that are creative, interesting, even game-like in nature, put a positive spin on studying, making it more motivating and productive to all students.

**Memory** strategies consist of any technique that aids *rote recitation* of learned material. Memory strategies are devised simply to recall elements without any attempt to understand the material more completely. A simple example of a memory strategy is the Alphabet Song learned by young children often long before they have any concept of letters. It is strictly a rote memory device—a mnemonic—and indeed, a very effective one.

Mnemonics in academia are created, often by individual students, to help remember rules, key words, lists, and categories. Memory strategies such as poems, songs, acronyms, sentences (the first letter of each word in the sentence is the same as an item in an ordered list), and word patterns are very effective in triggering the recall of a much larger body of information that has been learned through cognitive approaches. English language learners can even use their native language to design their own memory devices. When students recognize the efficiency of mnemonics as a recall tool and feel comfortable using them, you can assign the creation of a mnemonic as an unusual and enjoyable homework assignment (Figure 4.1).

### Examples of Familiar Mnemonics

- The "I before E" poem to recall spelling rules
- The poem and the "knuckle technique" of remembering which months of the year have fewer than 30 days (Figure 4.2)
- The "tricks" of the multiplication table (Figure 4.3)
- The made-up word to remember the color spectrum in which the letters recall the colors in their correct order (Figure 4.4)
- The silly sentences to remember the names of the strings on a guitar and the order of the planets in our solar system (Figure 4.4)

> Ask students to create a mnemonic designed to recall the elements in a set of information. The mnemonic can be an acronym that sounds good or a silly sentence that works.
>
> Students will really have to process the content under study to complete this assignment, but they'll hardly know they're doing it!

**FIGURE 4.1. Assign a mnemonic for homework—it's challenging, fun, and effective!**

### You May Know the Poem
> Thirty days hath September
> April, June, and November
> All the rest have thirty-one
> Excepting February alone
> It has twenty-eight days time
> And each leap year twenty-nine

### But Do You Know the Knuckle Technique?
Hold your hand forward, palm down, and make a fist.

Starting with the knuckle above the index finger, count off the months, naming a month as you touch each knuckle *and space* between the knuckles. When you get to July at the pinky knuckle, touch that knuckle again for August, and reverse direction.

Have you noticed that all the months that fall into the spaces have fewer than 31 days?

**FIGURE 4.2. Two Mnemonics to Remember the Number of Days in the Months**

### The 9 Times Trick

Hold both hands in front of you with your fingers spread out.

For 9 × 3 bend your third finger on your left hand down.
(9 × 4 would be the fourth finger, and so on)

You have 2 fingers in front of the bent finger and 7 after the bent finger,

And there's the answer: 27.

This technique works for the 9 times tables up to 10.

### The 4 Times Trick

For this one, you only need to know how to double a number.

Simply, double a number, and then double it again!

### The 11 Times Trick

To multiply 11 by any two-digit number:

*Example 1*

Multiply 11 by 18. Jot down 1 and 8 with a space between it: 1 8.

Add the 1 and the 8 and put that number in the middle: 198.

11 × 18 = 198

*Example 2*

When the digits of the multiplier add up to 10 or more, do it this way:

Multiply 11 by 39. Jot down 3 and 9 with a space between it: 3 9.

Add the 3 and the 9 to get 12.

Put the 2 in the middle between the 3 and the 9, then add the 1 to the 3:

$$\begin{array}{c} 4 \\ \cancel{3}29 \\ 11 \times 39 = 429 \end{array}$$

**FIGURE 4.3. Multiplication Mnemonics**

---

**For the Color Spectrum**

"Roy–G–Biv" = red, orange, yellow, green, blue, indigo, violet

**For the Notes of the Strings of the Guitar**

E–G–B–D–F = Every good boy does fine.
                    Every good boy deserves fudge.

**For the Order of the Planets**

Mercury–Venus–Earth–Mars–Jupiter–Saturn–Uranus–Neptune–Pluto =
My very excellent mother just served us nine pizzas.
or
My very excellent mother just showed us nine planets.

---

**FIGURE 4.4. More Mnemonics**

**Social** strategies are those in which the learner works with one or more other students or simply learns from the environment. Because these strategies are, as the name states, social, they often feel less like practice and more like fun.

*Examples of Social Strategies*

- Working in class in pairs or small groups to clarify content, solve problems, and complete projects
- Playing teacher-made or professionally designed games to sharpen skills
- Asking questions and making requests (Figure 4.5, page 37)
- Doing homework with a friend
- Studying with a partner for a test
- Watching select television programs
- Observing peers to learn more about culture and language

**Compensation** strategies are techniques used to make up for something that isn't known or immediately accessible from memory. We, as proficient speakers of English, regularly use this type of strategy in conversation when we use expressions like the *whatchamacallit,* the *thingamajiggy,* or just plain *that thing . . . you know what I mean.* We are using a word or phrase to replace the one we are searching for but cannot find at that moment—a compensation strategy.

Please say that again.

Could you write that word on the board, please?

Could you speak more slowly? I can understand better.

**FIGURE 4.5.  Questions and Requests: A Social Strategy That
English Language Learners Need to Know**

*Examples of Compensation Strategies*
- Stalling for time while we think of an appropriate response
- Making an educated guess that extends and generalizes what we know to what we don't know
- Using circumlocution—using a substitute phrase that "talks around" the word we don't know or "writes around" the word we can't spell

Figure 4.6 on page 38 offers specific usages of each of these compensation strategies. Encouraging your English language learners to develop and use compensation strategies may go a long way toward making them feel more willing to participate in class.

## It's Good to Mix and Match Strategies

While all students need to use a variety of strategy types, English language learners in particular will learn more effectively from using strategies in combination. Cognitive strategies used together with social strategies offer English language learners the added support of negotiated learning and increase their possibilities for success. Understanding the potential of each of the strategy types, alone and in combination, can help teachers provide the best opportunities for strategy training in the classroom.

## TEACHING LEARNING STRATEGIES

## Teach Strategies Explicitly

You may already be aware that strategy training should not be subtle. It needs to be taught explicitly and overtly. For students to recognize the usefulness of learning strategies in general, specific strategies need to be directly tied to learning specific content.

**Stalling for Time**

- Repeating the question or statement

- Using fillers like *Well, . . .* or *Hmmm . . .*

- Using expressions like *"That's a tough question"* or *"That's a complicated issue"*

- Coughing or clearing your throat

- Using any combination of the above

**Making Educated Guesses**

- Using *airplane driver* as an extension of known expressions, like *truck driver* and *taxi driver*, when the word *pilot* is not known

**Using Circumlocutions**

- Using the descriptive phrase *the man who drives the airplane*, instead of the unknown word *pilot*

- Using the phrase *the machine that makes the bread dark*, in place of the unknown word *toaster*

**FIGURE 4.6. Examples of Compensation Strategies**

Strategy teaching is a four-step process (see Figure 4.7). First, introduce the strategy to your students and *label* it as a new learning strategy. Next, *identify* it by name, and explain how it is used. Then, *demonstrate* its application to the specific content under study. Finally, give students the time and opportunity to *practice* using it.

And how exactly do you explicitly *teach* learning strategies? Thinking aloud or modeling is a very effective training approach. You, the teacher-as-student,

**1.** Introduce it and label it as a new strategy.

**2.** Identify it by name.

**3.** Demonstrate how to use it.

**4.** Give students time and opportunity for practice.

**FIGURE 4.7. Strategy Teaching in Four Steps**

**Your student correctly infers information from the text:**

ASK: *Where did you find the information that helped you with that answer?*

**Your student solves a complex problem:**

ASK: *How did you arrive at that answer?*

**Your student presents an informed opinion on a topic:**

ASK: *What information led you to this opinion?*

**Your student gets a good grade on a test:**

ASK: *How exactly did you study for this test?*

**FIGURE 4.8. Think-Aloud Applications for Strategy Training**

might say something like, "If I had to learn this, I would probably . . . ," giving a detailed, step-by-step description of the *process* you would use. You are, in effect, modeling the "how-to" of learning.

Another approach to the think-aloud technique is to ask students how they themselves learn. Guided questions such as those in Figure 4.8 about how they knew or learned specific information will allow them to model their own strategies of learning. If you should hear a unique approach to learning, you can label that strategy with the name of the student who contributed it. Imagine how nice it feels to have a strategy named for you! Additional techniques for strategy training can include explanation, handouts, activities, and brainstorming.

Teachers can help students identify their own current learning strategies through survey questions and discussion. One helpful technique is to make a display naming the strategies and showing how they are used. As each new strategy is taught, add it to the poster or bulletin board. Students themselves can keep a learning strategy log or journal. In either case, students will have a ready reference—a menu or guide—from which to draw. Class and home assignments might frequently include a brief discussion of which strategies would be most appropriate, effective, and efficient to achieve a successful outcome.

## A NOTE ABOUT LEARNING STRATEGIES AND TEACHING STRATEGIES

Learning strategies and teaching strategies are *not* the same thing. Learning strategies are used *by the student* to understand, retain, and apply new knowledge. They are not readily visible or immediately identifiable.

Teaching strategies are used *by the teacher* to facilitate understanding of knowledge and to make content more accessible to students. These are the techniques, approaches, activities, and assignments that teachers use to help students understand and learn the information. They are immediately visible and identifiable; indeed, they are what administrators look for when they do classroom observations. The subset of teaching strategies used for English language learners is part of *scaffolded instruction*.

Return now to the short vignette at the beginning of this chapter about Rosalia. What strategies can she and her ELL peers use to find answers to those confusing math word problems? Figure 4.9 describes the process of *streamlining*, a series of cognitive and social learning strategies that offer ELLs a good point to start working on the solutions.

This book presents an abundance of both learning strategies and teaching strategies. All the strategies are easy to implement. They are designed to fit right in with your curriculum as you now teach it. They are designed for immediate use by you, the content teacher, who strives for increased success for the English language learners in your classroom.

---

### Step 1: Make language substitutions.

In pairs or small groups, look for words or phrases that can be replaced with more simple language.

### Step 2: Determine the information presented.

Reread the now-simplified wording of the problem. Search out and write down all information given in the problem.

### Step 3: Determine information needed for solution.

Look for words that offer clues to the information needed in the solution. Look for words that show how to process the information presented.

### Step 4: Determine the process needed for solution.

Using the words or phrases from Step 3, figure out the process needed to find the solution.

### Step 5: Solve the problem.

---

**FIGURE 4.9. Streamlining: A Learning Strategy to Help Rosalia Solve Math Word Problems**

# CHAPTER 5

# Textbook Strategies

The written language of content instruction is a challenge for English language learners. Textbooks contain highly abstract and cognitively demanding concepts, and they are written in language appropriate to the grade for which they are intended. Fortunately, textbook readings can be made more comprehensible to English language learners—and to native English-speaking students who do not read at grade level—through the creative application of modification strategies.

## MAKE THE MOST OF YOUR TEXTBOOK

Teachers usually have little control over which textbooks they use in their classrooms. In most school districts, teachers simply use the ones they are given and generally find them acceptable, as today's textbooks tend to be user-friendly and engaging for students. Students who are English language learners, however, may view even the best of these with apprehension. Their reading skills in English are not yet sufficiently developed to comprehend grade-level textbook materials. For them, reading content-area textbooks is often a frustrating experience. The amount of information may appear overwhelming. The time and effort they spend trying to make it understandable often bring few rewards and little satisfaction. Incorporating some of the ideas that follow will help make the class textbook more comprehensible for these students.

### Teach Students to Use Textbook Aids

Many students are unaware of the existence of textbook aids as a resource to help them understand the information in the text. One student actually came to his teacher in January, *five months after the school year had begun*, and said, "Our textbook has a bilingual dictionary in the back! Did you know that?" There is no doubt that this student would have benefitted had he made use of this resource during the first half of the year as well. Students who know which textbook aids are available to them and who understand how to use them have an immediate advantage.

Using textbook aids is an important learning strategy and should be taught explicitly whenever a new textbook is introduced. You can teach students how to use these aids by explicitly presenting them. Or you can try a discovery approach, giving your students a list of aids and having them work in groups to identify and locate examples of each item in their textbooks. In a follow-up discussion, explain the purpose of each item and how to use it to its best advantage.

### Contents and Index

The Contents and Index serve as shortcuts to locating specific information contained in a text. A simple technique to teach the usefulness of these aids is to give grouped students a list of topics and have them note the page number(s) in the text where information is given. They might also note whether they used the Contents or the Index. Try turning this practice activity into a game: Give it an intriguing name like *Textbook Sleuths*, add a time factor, and make it a competition.

### Chapter Titles, Section Headings, and Subsection Headings

Titles and headings should be considered *clues* to help students organize their thinking about the type of information that follows. Section and subsection headings usually contain key words or phrases that highlight important facts or concepts. Teach students to scan headings and make associations as a regular *prereading* activity.

### Outlines and Questions

Textbooks often include outlines or questions at the beginning of each chapter and review questions at the end to highlight important information. As a prereading activity, they can be used to direct students' attention to concepts, ideas, and details presented in the chapter. As a postreading strategy, they allow students to check their comprehension (self-evaluation—a metacognitive learning strategy) and to engage in critical thinking.

### Chapter Summaries and Review Sections

Summaries and reviews form an important part of most of today's textbooks. They present key concepts and points of information at the ends of sections and chapters. The language used in summary and review segments is often more concise than that in the body of the text. It is a good strategy to teach your English language learners to read these segments *before* reading the section or chapter. Prereading the summaries or reviews helps students organize their thinking about the content they will soon read in the text. It allows them to form a foundation that facilitates comprehension of the concepts, facts, and details presented in the body of the text. It is a strategy that will benefit all students who find reading the text challenging.

## Glossaries

Textbook glossaries are a bonus feature for all students, and especially for English language learners. Make your students aware that the reason that words or phrases are highlighted in boldface or italic type in the body of the text is because they are important to understanding the concepts. These key words are explained or defined in a glossary at the end of the textbook, or written as a notation in the margin, or listed at the beginning or end of the chapter. Because most textbooks do not include a bilingual glossary, English language learners should be encouraged to make liberal use of *bilingual dictionaries* for additional clarification.

The textbook aids in the next group are particularly valuable to those students whose English language skills are at the beginner or low-intermediate level. These aids give information in a less linguistically demanding way.

## Text Boxes and Highlighted Areas

Text boxes and highlighted areas focus on key concepts. They often present information in more concise language, or give examples to clarify concepts.

## Text Organizers

Text organizers include elements such as bulleted or numbered lists, and sentences written in bold print or different colored ink. Students should realize that these elements are there to indicate that this information is important.

## Graphics

Graphics in textbooks present information in chart, table, or diagram formats. They increase comprehensibility by visually contextualizing the printed words. English language learners can derive a great deal of information by learning to analyze the information displayed in these charts, tables, and diagrams.

## Visuals

Visuals in textbooks are designed to appeal to students, to capture their attention, to offer them contextual support, and sometimes to enrich their understanding of concepts presented in the text. As with graphics, students should understand that they are not merely decoration: indeed, real information is offered in the maps, pictures, and illustrations included in the text. English language learners and below-level readers should be encouraged first to scan visuals to activate or build background knowledge, and then to use them in conjunction with written text to help clarify meaning.

No single textbook will contain all of these aids to comprehension, but all textbooks contain some. Use a class session at the beginning of the term to teach your students how to use the aids available in their textbook. Or try the unusual approach to becoming familiar with textbooks described in Figure 5.1. Either way, you will give your students a set of valuable tools they will use throughout the school year.

On the first day of school, Ms. Molvig, a middle school science teacher, spent the period talking about the course that lay ahead. The class ended with the homework assignment, "Familiarize yourselves with your textbook." What the students heard, of course, was, "No homework."

The next day as class began, Ms. Molvig told the class to clear their desks, take out a piece of paper, write their names at the top, and number it 1 through 10. The students gave each other puzzled looks. A quiz? How could they have a quiz when they didn't even have any homework?

The first question on the quiz was "What is the name of your text book?" Other questions followed such as "What information is given at the end of each chapter?" and "Does your textbook have a glossary?"

Correcting the quiz was Ms. Molvig's way of assuring that the students and their textbooks became well acquainted. The students in this science class learned a valuable lesson in class that day— about their textbook and about their teacher.

**FIGURE 5.1. True Tale: How to Teach Textbook Aids**

## Preselect and Preteach Vocabulary

Ask English language learners of all ages what they think is the key to understanding English, and about 75% will answer, "vocabulary." It is difficult to argue against this point of view: Knowing what words mean is unquestionably critical to comprehension.

Textbooks and their accompanying teachers' editions do a creditable job of identifying and defining new vocabulary that appears in each chapter. These words are content-specific or technical in nature; they are the words students must learn in order to understand the concepts that follow. If it were only these words that needed explanation, teachers and students would have an easy task.

Other than obvious technical or content-specific vocabulary in textbooks, there are four other categories of words that may be unknown or misunderstood by English language learners. These are (1) new usages of familiar words, (2) synonyms, (3) idioms, and (4) just plain new words.

### New Usages of Familiar Words

Think of the word *strike*. In what context might students be familiar with this word? Did you think of baseball? Depending on your interests, you might also have thought of bowling or fishing. These are the contexts in which the word *strike* is most often used. In conversation, *strike* is a word of multiple meanings. Here are just a few:

Police thought the murderer would **strike** again.

He tried to **strike** the match.

A brilliant idea suddenly **struck** him.

The clock **struck** two.

The dog was **struck** by a car.

**Strike** it rich.

**Strike** while the iron is hot.

He tried unsuccessfully to **strike** up a conversation.

In textbooks, however, the word *strike* appears in wholly different contexts. Think now of how it relates to:

Industry—The workers went on **strike.**

Mining—The prospectors were hoping to **strike** gold.

Weather—Lightning can **strike** before a storm.

Military—The air **strike** was considered successful.

English language learners need to understand that a single word can have multiple meanings depending on context. You can help them by scanning the text for words that might be misunderstood. Look for words that may be confusing because they would be more commonly known with a different meaning in a more conversational or social context. Figure 5.2 is a true story of a misunderstanding of this type.

In math and science in particular, common conversational words are used to denote totally different concepts. Look for potentially confusing words like these:

| *Science* | *Math* |
|---|---|
| energy | table |
| mass | round |
| matter | root |
| force | power |
| kingdom | product |

### Synonyms

Synonyms add interest and sophistication to writing. They also add another source of confusion for English language learners. Consider the number of synonymous phrases we use to talk about this simple arithmetic problem:

A second-grade teacher of a self-contained ESL class asked her class why they thought that Christopher Columbus, with his few men, was able to conquer many thousands of Native Indians living in the islands of the Caribbean. When none of them answered, she explained. "It's because Christopher Columbus and his men had arms and the Native Indians didn't have any."

Continuing the discussion, she asked what kind of life the Caribbean Indians had before being conquered by Columbus. One student answered, "Very hard," as all the others nodded their heads in agreement.

Surprised by this response, she asked, "How could it have been a hard life? They had beautiful warm weather, lots of food to eat, especially fruits and vegetables. They didn't need to wear a lot of clothing or build strong houses to keep out the cold. Why do you think they had a hard life?"

One student timidly offered an explanation—"Because they had no arms! How could they do anything?"

**FIGURE 5.2. True Tale: A Complete Misunderstanding**

$$8 \\ -\,5$$

Subtract 5 from 8.

Take 5 away from 8.

Take away 5 from 8.

8 minus 5 equals . . . ?

8 less 5 equals . . . ?

5 from 8 equals . . . ?

The words we use to talk about something may be entirely different from the wording used in the textbook.

At a more advanced level, think about the different words and phrases that are used to represent the concept of *freedom* in written texts. A search through several high school social studies textbooks produced the following list:

| | | |
|---|---|---|
| autonomy | liberation | self-reliance |
| emancipation | liberty | self-sufficiency |
| home rule | self-determination | sovereignty |
| independence | self-government | |

Teachers can lighten the vocabulary load on English language learners by pointing out, in advance of the reading assignment, the variety of words that relate to the concept, explaining in this particular instance that they all refer to the basic concept of *freedom*.

### Idioms

English language learners love to learn idioms because they feel, and perhaps rightly so, that if they understand idioms, they *really* know English. Idioms are groups of words whose meaning is unrelated to knowledge of the actual words. Idioms are more than the sum of their parts. Analyzing idioms on a word-by-word basis can produce some odd images. Visualize the literal meaning of these widely used idiomatic expressions:

She really put her foot in her mouth.

It's raining cats and dogs.

I'm all ears.

He's got two left feet.

Idiomatic expressions are used in academic writing as well. The phrases in Figure 5.3 are frequent references in social studies textbooks. Can you imagine an English language learner thinking, "Why did they stand under a flag to fight?"

Native speakers and writers of English use idioms generously and unconsciously. Teachers can help their English language learners by scanning a text for idiomatic usages and references. It might even make an interesting extra credit assignment to give to some of the more advanced students in the class.

### New Words

This is the catchall category—the least well-defined, the most individualized, and the most challenging for the teacher. Here are some ideas to help you and your students determine and define words that may need some extra attention.

| About the Civil War | About the American Flag |
|---|---|
| a house divided | the Stars and Stripes |
| fighting under the Confederate flag | Old Glory |
| on the homefront | the Red, White, and Blue |
| loss of lives | |

**FIGURE 5.3. Idiomatic References in Social Studies Textbooks**

*Turn your students into "language detectives."* This is a wonderful strategy for students whose native language is Spanish or one of the other Latin root languages. This strategy works because of an event that took place in the year 1066.

In that year, the Normans from France conquered the Angles and Saxons living in what is now England. Because they were conquerors, the Norman language, an early version of today's French, became the language of position and power. It also became the language of academia. The conquered Anglo-Saxons continued using their own language in everyday life, and a duality was created that still exists in the English that we use today.

Many academic words in English—words that cut across all academic disciplines—come from the old Norman French, which itself has its roots in ancient Greek and Latin. The common words used in social, spoken English derive from Anglo-Saxon roots. So, we often speak and hear different words in conversation than we read and write in school. Figure 5.4 gives several examples of word usages in conversational English and academic English.

You can use this information to help your Spanish speakers, whose language is also based on Latin-Greek roots, to become "language detectives." Spanish speakers can use the database of their native language to increase their reading comprehension by scanning a text for academic words with Spanish cognates (Figure 5.5). They can even share their discoveries with the rest of the class. It becomes a win-win situation.

*Have students develop a personal dictionary.* Personal dictionaries are a valuable strategy to help students remember words that they find academically useful and/or personally interesting. You or the students can select an organizing principle—subject specific, alphabetical, parts of speech, general/technical, or social/academic. Dictionaries can be monolingual or bilingual. English language

| Conversational English | Academic English |
| --- | --- |
| Did you *meet* anyone at the store today? | The troops *encountered* no resistance. |
| Get in *line.* | Arrange the numbers in *sequence.* |
| Let's *build* a castle. | The troops planned to *construct* a bridge. |
| The vacation *lasted* two full weeks. | The people *endured* two centuries of tyranny. |
| The salad was *enough* for two people. | The supplies were *sufficient* for only a week. |

**FIGURE 5.4. Comparison of Conversational English and Academic English**

| Academic Word | Spanish Word | Common Word |
|---|---|---|
| encounter | encontrar | meet |
| observe | observar | watch |
| maintain | mantener | keep |
| ultimate | último | last |
| equal | igual | same |
| entire | entero | whole |
| quantity | cantidad | amount |

**FIGURE 5.5. Turn your Spanish speakers into "language detectives"**

learners at the beginner's level can use the vocabulary circle as an entry (Figure 5.6). Additional possibilities for inclusion in the circle, or as a column entry in personal dictionaries, are native language translations, synonyms, or antonyms. It

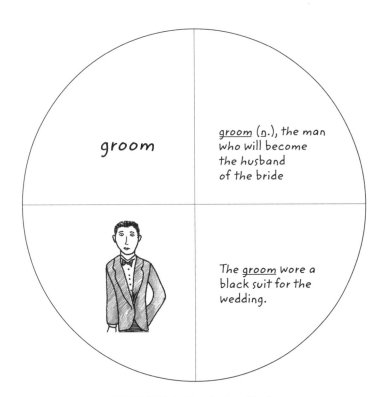

**FIGURE 5.6. Vocabulary Circle**

| New Word 📖 | Goes with . . . ☺ | But not . . . ☹ |
|---|---|---|
| bargain | fair bargain | balanced, just |
| | hard bargain | firm, stiff, rigid |
| trick | clever trick | bright, smart, intelligent |
| | dirty trick | dishonest, crooked, unclean, soiled |

**FIGURE 5.7. Examples of Collocations**

may also be helpful to include a section for collocations—words that commonly appear in combination with the entry word. ELLs need to learn word associations that come so naturally to native speakers who know, for example, that air can be heavy with *humidity* but *thick* with smoke, and *thin*, never *slim* or *skinny*, at high altitudes. Figure 5.7 offers additional examples of collocated usages in a format suitable for students to use. Personal dictionaries benefit all students. They are a valuable, easy-to-use tool for building vocabulary.

*Demonstrate the value of a student-friendly dictionary.* Have you ever looked up a word in the dictionary and, after reading the definition, found you still had no idea of what the word meant? Now imagine, if *you* had difficulty with the meaning, what a challenge it would be for an English language learner!

Student dictionaries are available at beginner, intermediate, and advanced levels. In the Longman series of dictionaries, the vocabulary used in the definitions is based on the 2000 most commonly used words in the English language. Compare the clarity of the definitions shown in Figure 5.8. It is immediately apparent that the student dictionary definition is linguistically easier to understand.

Student dictionaries also simplify definitions by listing each meaning of a word as a separate entry, and by using it in a sentence. Additionally, they offer usage notes, synonyms and antonyms, examples, and illustrations and pictures. At the more advanced level, student dictionaries label words as approving or disapproving (think about the subtle differences between the words *thin/slim/skinny* or *childish/childlike*, for example), formal, literary or old-fashioned, informal, humorous, slang or nonstandard, and even offensive or taboo. Idiomatic expressions, collocations, and frequency information for spoken and written words are presented as well.

Student dictionaries serve as a valuable aid to teachers as well. The clarity of the depth and breadth of information they contain helps teachers in their preparation of any type of vocabulary work. Your classroom should have at least one student dictionary. You and your students will find yourselves reaching for it on a regular basis.

---

**Longman's Basic Dictionary v. Webster's Tenth Collegiate Dictionary**

**"landlady"**

*Longman's:* a woman who owns a building and rents it to others

*Webster's:*  a woman who is a landlord

**"landlord"**

*Longman's:* someone who owns a building and rents it to others

*Webster's:*  the owner of property (as land, houses, or apartments) that is leased or rented to another; the master of an inn or lodging house (innkeeper)

---

**FIGURE 5.8. Comparison of Dictionary Definitions**

*Use a text analysis Website to determine which words to teach.* A text analysis Website can help you decide which words, of all the many in a text passage, you really need to teach. It is an awesome tool.

One such website, called *The Compleat Lexical Tutor*, has been developed by the Université de Québec à Montréal. It is designed to create a vocabulary profile of any text you input. You can find it at this Web address:

http://www.er.uqam.ca/nobel/r21270/cgi-bin/webfreqs/web_vp.cgi

You can also do a search for it by name.

The website presents you with a box to type or scan in the desired text. When you have completed inputting the text, click on the ⌐Submit window⌐ button, and in a matter of seconds, a color-coded vocabulary profile of the text appears on your computer screen. The color coding represents words of four different frequency types. For purposes of this book, the colors have been changed to different font styles and underlining.

K1 (regular text): the most frequent 1000 word families

K2 (underline): the second 1000 most frequent word families

AWL (boldfaced italics): Academic Word List, or words that are common to all subject domains

Off-List Words (boldfaced roman): topic-specific, technical, and/or infrequently used; also dates, place names, and names of people

The easiest way to understand the wonders of this Web tool is to look at an actual example from a high school–level social studies textbook, *The American Nation* (J. W. Davidson, Prentice Hall, 2003: p. 510). Figure 5.9 shows the original passage as it appears in the textbook. In Figure 5.10, the same passage has been inserted into the box and is ready to be submitted. When the vocabulary profile is returned, as shown in Figure 5.11, the black-printed passage now appears coded with a complete analysis of word counts and other linguistic data. Finally, Figure 5.12 shows the actual listings of words in each of the four frequency categories.

You may now be thinking, "Interesting, yes. But now what? What useful information can be gathered from this data?"

The first piece of valuable information is that more than 80% of the words (217 of 259) are in the K1 category, words already most likely known by English language learners. You can safely assume that those 217 words are currently part of your ELL students' working vocabularies.

Next, look at the words included in the Off-List category in Figure 5.12. Of the nineteen words, thirteen are proper nouns. The six words remaining are *confederation, dedicated, prophetic, rending, secede,* and *toll.* Add these to the thirteen K2 word families and the six AWL families, and the grand total of possible "difficult" words for your English language learners is twenty-five. That's twenty-five words of the original 259 in the passage, or about 10%, and a glance at those words, shown in Figure 5.13, will assure you that some of them will already be known. It should come as a comforting thought to know that your students can handle more than 90% of the words in this passage. Only the small number of remaining words are the ones you and your students need to focus on to increase their understanding of concepts.

So what can this website do for you? It helps you, the content teacher, narrow the challenge of "so many words, so little time." Try it—it's amazing!

As the Confederates surrendered, Union soldiers began to cheer. Grant ordered them to be silent. "The war is over," he said. "The rebels are our countrymen again."

## A Turning Point in American History

The toll of the Civil War was immense. More than 360,000 Union soldiers and 250,000 Confederate soldiers lost their lives. No war has ever resulted in more American deaths. In dollars, the war's cost was about 20 billion. That was more than 11 times the entire amount spent by the federal government between 1789 and 1861!

The Civil War was a major turning point in American history. The balance of power was changed. The Democratic party lost its influence and the Republicans were in a commanding position. No longer would Americans speak of the nation as a confederation of states. Before the war, Americans referred to "*these* United States." After, they began speaking of "*the* United States." The idea that each state might secede, if it chose, was dead. As a result, the power of the federal government grew.

The war also put an end to slavery in the United States. For years, Americans had debated whether slavery could exist in a nation dedicated to the ideals of liberty and equality. By the war's end, millions of African Americans had gained their freedom. Millions more Americans, both North and South, began to think about what it meant to be free and equal.

To be sure, a long and difficult struggle for equality lay ahead. Yet, Lincoln's words at Gettysburg were prophetic: "We here highly resolve . . . that this nation, under God, shall have a new birth of freedom." From out of a cruel, bitter, often heart-rending war, the United States did indeed emerge a stronger, freer nation.

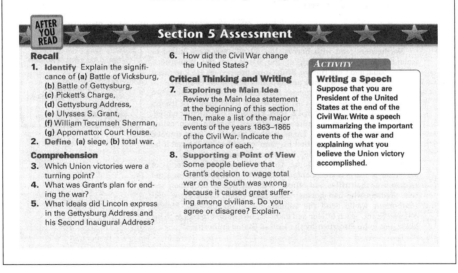

**AFTER YOU READ**

### Section 5 Assessment

**Recall**

**1. Identify** Explain the significance of **(a)** Battle of Vicksburg, **(b)** Battle of Gettysburg, **(c)** Pickett's Charge, **(d)** Gettysburg Address, **(e)** Ulysses S. Grant, **(f)** William Tecumseh Sherman, **(g)** Appomattox Court House.
**2. Define  (a)** siege, **(b)** total war.

**Comprehension**

**3.** Which Union victories were a turning point?
**4.** What was Grant's plan for ending the war?
**5.** What ideals did Lincoln express in the Gettysburg Address and his Second Inaugural Address?

**6.** How did the Civil War change the United States?

**Critical Thinking and Writing**

**7. Exploring the Main Idea** Review the Main Idea statement at the beginning of this section. Then, make a list of the major events of the years 1863–1865 of the Civil War. Indicate the importance of each.
**8. Supporting a Point of View** Some people believe that Grant's decision to wage total war on the South was wrong because it caused great suffering among civilians. Do you agree or disagree? Explain.

*ACTIVITY*

**Writing a Speech**
Suppose that you are President of the United States at the end of the Civil War. Write a speech summarizing the important events of the war and explaining what you believe the Union victory accomplished.

**FIGURE 5.9. Original Text Passage from *The American Nation* (J. W. Davidson, *The American Nation*, Prentice Hall, 2003, p.510)**

Web Vocabulary Profiler

Home > VocabProfile

# Web VP (v 1.5)

Type or paste a text below and click Submit_window to see its Frequency Profile.

**Title:** A Turning Point          | <u>FREQ</u> I <u>VP-CLOZE</u> I <u>RESEARCH</u> I <u>STUDENTS</u> I <u>FRENCH</u> I
<u>X$^2$</u> I <u>AWL texts</u>I

> The Toll of the Civil War was immense. More than 300,000 Union soldiers and 250,000 Confederate soldiers lost their lives. No war has ever resulted in more American deaths. In dollars, the war's cost was about 20 billion. That was more than 11 times the entire amount spent by the federal government between 1789 and 1861!
>     The Civil War was a major turning point in American history. The balance of power was changed. The Democratic party lost its influence and the Republicans were in a commanding position. No longer would Americans speak of the nation as a confederation of states. Before the war, Americans referred to "these United States." After, they began speaking of "the United States." The idea that each state might secede, if it chose, was dead. As a result, the power of the federal government grew.
>     The war also put an end to slavery in the United States.  For years, Americans had debated whether slavery could exist in a nation dedicated to the ideals of liberty and equality.  By the war's end, millions of African Americans had gained their freedom. Millions more Americans, both North and South, began to think about what it meant to be free and equal.
>     To be sure, a long and difficult struggle for equality lay ahead. Yet, Lincoln's words at Gettysburg were prophetic: "We here highly resolve...that this nation, under God, shall have a new birth of freedom." From out of a cruel, bitter, often heart-rending war, the United States did indeed emerge a stronger, freer nation.

Words to recategorize as high frequency (e.g. common names etc).   Output display:

None

☑ Family ☑ Subs *1k,AWL*

Table + Text + Lists: ☐ Token☐ Type

Samples: Isogram ILit(1) (2)ISci(1) (2)I News(1) (2)I Speech(1) (2) I  [ Highlight ]     [ Count words ]
[ **Submit_Window** ]

---

**OR...** [ **Browse...** ] your own drive and [ **Submit_file** ] to upload larger *.txt* files (to 150k words).

Original VP by P. Nation, VUW New Zealand & B. Laufer, U Haifa, Israel; AWL & sublists by A. Coxhead VUW; WebVP adapted by T. Cobb, UQAM Canada.

**FIGURE 5.10.  UQAM Website with Text Passage Ready for Analysis**

VP Online. . .

**Home > VocabProfile > VP output**

WEB VP OUTPUT FOR FILE: A Turning Point

**Recategorized words:** None

**Note:** In the output text, punctuation (but not sentence capitalization) is eliminated; figures (1, 20, etc) are replaced by the word *number*, contractions are replaced by constituent words; type-token ration is calculated using constituents; and in the 1k sub-analysis content + function words may sum to less than total (depending on user treatment of proper nouns, and program decision to class numbers as 1k although not contained in 1k list).

| | Families | Types | Tokens | Percent | | |
|---|---|---|---|---|---|---|
| First 500: | . . . | . . . | (183) | (70.66%) | Words in text (tokens): | 259 |
| K1 Words (1 to 1000): | 96 | 113 | **218** | **84.17%** | Different words (types): | 146 |
| | | | | | Type-token ratio: | 0.56 |
| Function: | . . . | . . . | (112) | (43.24%) | (Tokens per type: | 1.77) |
| Content: | . . . | . . . | (106) | (40.93%) | Function-content ratio: | 0.43 |
| K2 Words (1001 to 2000): | 13 | 13 | **14** | **5.41%** | Onlist Tokens: | 240 |
| | | | | | Onlist Types: | 132 |
| *AWL Words (academic):* | 6 | 6 | **8** | **3.09%** | Onlist Type-Token: | 0.55 |
| | | | | | Onlist Families: | 115 |
| **Off-List Words:** | ? | 14 | **19** | **7.34%** | Onlist Family/token: | 0.48 |
| | | | | | Onlist Family/type: | 0.87 |
| | 115+? | 146 | 259 | 100% | | |

Output text: The **Toll** of the *Civil* War was <u>immense</u> More than number number Union soldiers and number number **Confederate** soldiers lost their lives No war has ever resulted in more **American** deaths In dollars the war cost was about number <u>billion</u> That was more than number times the <u>entire</u> amount spent by the *federal* <u>government</u> between number and number The *Civil* War was a *major* turning point in **American** history The <u>balance</u> of power was changed The **Democratic** party lost its influence and the Republicans were in a commanding position No longer would **Americans** speak of the nation as a **confederation** of states Before the war **Americans** <u>referred</u> to these United States After they began speaking of the United States The idea that each state might **secede** if it chose was dead As a result the power of the *federal* <u>government</u> grew The war also put an end to <u>slavery</u> in the United States For years **Americans** had debated whether <u>slavery</u> could exist in a nation **dedicated** to the <u>ideals</u> of <u>liberty</u> and equality By the war end millions of **African Americans** had gained their freedom Millions more **Americans** both North and South began to think about what it meant to be free and equal To be sure a long and difficult struggle for equality lay <u>ahead</u> Yet **Lincoln** words at **Gettysburg** were **prophetic** We here highly *resolve* that this nation under God shall have a new <u>birth</u> of freedom From out of a <u>cruel</u> <u>bitter</u> often heart **rending** war the United States did indeed *emerge* a stronger freer nation

**FIGURE 5.11. UQAM Website Showing Completed Vocabulary Profile**

VP Online. . .
**1001-2000 [13:13:14]** <u>ahead balance billion birth bitter cruel entire government ideals immense liberty referred slavery slavery</u>

**AWL [6:6:8]** *civil civil debated emerge federal federal major resolve*

**Sublist 1**
*major*

**Sublist 4**
*civil civil debated emerge resolve*

**Sublist 6**
*federal federal*

**OFF LIST [?:14:19]** african american american americans americans americans americans americans confederate confederation dedicated democratic gettysburg government lincoln prophetic rending secede toll

**Family List**
family_[number of tokens]

1k families: [families 96: types 113: tokens 218] a_[10] about_[2] after_[1] also_[1] amount_[1] and_[7] as_[2] at_[1] be_[10] before_[1] begin_[2] between_[1] both_[1] by_[2] change_[1] choose_[1] command_[1] cost_[1] could_[1] dead_[2] difficult_[1] do_[1] dollar_[1] each_[1] end_[2] equal_[3] ever_[1] exist_[1] father_[6] for_[2] free_[4] from_[1] gain_[1] god_[1] grow_[1] have_[4] heart_[1] here_[1] high_[1] history_[1] idea_[1] if_[1] indeed_[1] influence_[1] it_[3] lay_[1] live_[1] long_[2] lose_[2] mean_[1] might_[1] million_[2] more_[4] nation_[4] new_[1] no_[2] north_[1] number_[8] of_[10] often_[1] out_[1] party_[1] point_[1] position_[1] power_[2] put_[1] republic_[1] result_[2] shall_[1] soldier_[2] south_[1] speak_[2] spend_[1] state_[6] strong_[1] struggle_[1] sure_[1] than_[2] the_[20] they_[3] think_[1] this_[5] time_[1] to_[6] turn_[1] under_[1] union_[1] unite_[4] war_[8] we_[1] what_[1] whether_[1] word_[1] would_[1] year_[1] yet_[1]

2k families: [13:13:14] <u>ahead_[1] balance_[1] billion_[1] birth_[1] bitter_[1] cruel_[1] entire_[1] govern_[1] ideal_[1] immense_[1] liberty_[1] refer_[1] slave_[2]</u>

AWL families: [6:6:8] *civil_[2] debate_[1] emerge_[1] federal_[2] major_[1] resolve_[1]*

**FIGURE 5.12.  UQAM Website Vocabulary Profile Word Lists**

| Off-List | K2 | | AWL |
|---|---|---|---|
| confederation | ahead | govern | civil |
| dedicated | balance | ideal | debate |
| prophetic | billion | immense | emerge |
| rending | birth | liberty | federal |
| secede | bitter | refer | major |
| toll | cruel | slave | resolve |
| | entire | | |

**FIGURE 5.13. Which Words to Teach?**

## MORE STRATEGIES FOR TEXTBOOK COMPREHENSION

In addition to textbook aids and vocabulary strategies as means of facilitating content comprehension, there are other types of strategies that can help your students learn the concepts presented in their textbooks.

### Highlight Important Concepts

Readers grasp concepts by mentally organizing them. English language learners, in particular, will find a text easier to read and learn if they have an overview of concepts *before* reading the chapter. An effective way to do this is to offer extra credit to native-speaking students who are willing to make and share an *outline* or *T-notes* of the chapter.

T-notes are really a simplified form of an outline (Figure 5.14). The left column represents a main idea, and the right column shows supporting details and/or examples. In Figure 5.15, T-notes outline the passage about the Civil War that was used in the vocabulary profile. For English language learners, following the organized presentation and concise language of the outline while reading the textbook facilitates the task of comprehending these concepts.

The T-note format is flexible and adapts easily to all subjects. Figure 5.16 uses this format to outline a segment on water quality from the textbook *Focus on Earth Science* (Prentice Hall, 2001: pp. 333–336).

T-notes are useful in other ways as well. They are an excellent way for students to develop note-taking skills. Prepare a set of T-notes in which main ideas have already been listed in the left column. Give your students an in-class or home assignment of completing the Details/Examples column. Students who

| Main Ideas | Details/Examples |
|---|---|
| 1. _____ | 1. _____ |
|  | 2. _____ |
|  | 3. _____ |
| 2. _____ | 1. _____ |
|  | 2. _____ |
|  | 3. _____ |

**FIGURE 5.14.  T-Note Format**

| The Civil War—A Turning Point in American History | |
|---|---|
| **Main Ideas** | **Details/Examples** |
| 1.  The Civil War was expensive in lives and money. | 1.  360,000 Union soldiers died. |
|  | 2.  250,000 Confederate soldiers died. |
|  | 3.  $20 billion spent. |
| 2.  The Civil War was a turning point. | 1.  The Democratic party got weaker. |
|  | 2.  The Republican party got stronger. |
|  | 3.  States lost some power. |
|  | 4.  The federal government got stronger. |
| 3.  The Civil War officially ended slavery. | 1.  Millions of African-Americans became free. |
|  | 2.  Millions of Americans thought about the meaning of "free and equal." |
| 4.  The Civil War didn't end the struggle for equality. | 1.  In the Gettysburg Address, Lincoln said that the nation must work hard in the fight for equality. |
|  | 2.  This struggle made the U.S. a stronger, freer country. |

**FIGURE 5.15.  T-Notes in Social Studies**

| Factors Affecting Water Quality | |
|---|---|
| Main Ideas | Details/Examples |
| 1. Appearance and taste | 1. cloudiness |
| | 2. odor |
| | 3. color |
| | 4. minerals and chemicals |
| 2. Acidity | 1. measured in pH—0 to 14 |
| | 2. pure water is neutral—7 pH |
| | 3. lower pH = more acid |
| | 4. higher pH = more base |
| 3. Hardness | 1. based on 2 minerals—calcium and magnesium |
| | 2. hard water doesn't make suds |
| | 3. deposits from hard water clog water pipes and machines |
| 4. Disease-causing agents | 1. contamination from E. coli bacteria |
| | 2. comes from human and animal wastes |
| 5. Standards of quality | 1. set by the EPA |
| | 2. standards set concentration limits |
| | 3. concentration = amount of 1 substance in a certain amount of another substance |
| | 4. example: alphabet soup—number of letters per liter of soup |

**FIGURE 5.16. T-Notes in Science**

are new to the use of T-notes or those with low-level note-taking skills will benefit from seeing one or two items included in the Details/Examples column as a model of what to do.

T-notes serve as a reference and an aid to learning not only during the reading process but also later as a review. Students can use them individually, in pairs, or in small groups to study for an exam.

T-notes are a powerful strategy that helps to streamline the reading/learning process. They are user-friendly—easy to learn and readily adaptable to multiple tasks. T-notes are a cognitive learning strategy that, once learned, can be used in all content areas. They can become a useful tool for all the students in all their classes.

## Group Students to Discuss the Text

Reading, especially reading assigned as homework, has traditionally been viewed as an individual activity. Students generally read at home and are expected to arrive in class the next day prepared to discuss the material. In class, however, the teacher's questions often fall flat, and discussions turn out to be considerably less lively than planned. It seems that the students either didn't read the text or didn't understand it.

One way to increase responsiveness is to have the students discuss the assigned reading in groups for the first five or ten minutes of class. Maximize the productivity of these few minutes of group work by giving students several questions about key concepts, either written on the board or waiting on the students' desks. These questions help students organize their thinking. Focusing on important concepts readies the students for the rest of the lesson and promotes participation in class discussion.

English language learners will benefit enormously from the short time spent doing group work. Small-group discussion facilitates comprehension by enriching context. The giv-and-take of discussion affords English language learners—actually, *all* students—the opportunity to negotiate their knowledge and increase their understanding of information in the printed text.

## Record the Text

It has been well established that reading comprehension and retention rise when readers simultaneously see and hear information. Closed-captioned video has been proven an effective technique for developing reading skills both for nonnative speakers and for preliterate native speaking adults. Interestingly, one way that a good reader attempts to comprehend a difficult text is by reading the passage aloud. Hearing the printed words, even when you are reading them to yourself, assists in producing meaning.

English language learners benefit from seeing and hearing text in other ways as well. They learn pronunciation of unfamiliar words. They may make new associations of words in their oral and written forms, words that they may know in spoken form but not recognize in writing because they are spelled so differently from the way they are pronounced. And a final advantage concerns *homophones*, words that are pronounced the same but are spelled differently and have different meanings—*there–their–they're*, for example. Simultaneously seeing and hearing these words in context may help students to understand and remember the different meanings and usages.

Again for extra credit, students in your class can record entire chapters or important sections of the textbook. A bonus here is that the readers are actually reinforcing their own learning while helping others (*and* getting extra credit for it at the same time). Language learners can listen to the tape while reading the text, at home if possible or if not, in school. Using this multimedia approach facilitates comprehension.

## Use Learning Logs

Learning logs are structured content journals based on reading assignments from the textbook. Students use them while they are attempting to complete assigned pages. Figures 5.17 and 5.18 show two formats for learning logs. The positive phrasing of the last columns—phrases like "Questions I Have," "Things I Want to Know," and "Clueless"—are more student-friendly and less self-stigmatizing than the more traditional "What I Didn't Understand."

| Text Pages | What I Understood | New or Difficult Vocabulary | Questions I Have |
|---|---|---|---|
| | | | |

**FIGURE 5.17. Format of a Learning Log**

| Text Pages | I Get It | I Think I Get It | I Don't Have a Clue |
|---|---|---|---|
|  |  |  |  |

**FIGURE 5.18. Alternative Format for Learning Logs**

Because of the way that learning logs are structured, it is important to set aside a few minutes of class time to address the issues, questions, or difficulties that the students have noted in their logs. Students can meet in small groups to discuss their entries. They can help each other by exchanging understandings, answering each other's questions, and clarifying vocabulary. Encourage their independence, but offer your support as needed. Students should note in their logs the new understandings that result from these discussions.

Learning logs give language-learning students another way to become engaged in the process of negotiating knowledge and increasing their understanding of the text. The entries in students' learning logs also provide an excellent source of information for ongoing or summary review of the material.

Learning logs, like T-notes, are highly adaptable and can be used by students for a wide range of activities beyond text readings. In science, for example, the first column could be changed for use with in-class experiments or demonstrations. In math, learning logs may be useful during lessons in which new concepts or applications are presented. In all subject areas, learning logs can be used when videos or other media are used to contextualize or enrich understandings. The uses of learning logs are limited only by the imagination and creativity of the teacher.

## TWO STRATEGIES FOR REAL BEGINNERS

Teachers often ask what to do with the true English language beginner in class. How can a grade-level textbook be used by a newcomer who has just begun to learn English? The answer is as obvious as it is unsatisfying: an English language beginning-level learner cannot successfully use a grade-level textbook. There are, however, some approaches that may help students gain some knowledge of content while they are developing their English language skills.

## Volunteer Buddies

In almost every class, there are students who are "natural nurturers." Pair them with English language beginners to create a volunteer buddy system, a win-win situation for both sides. Beginners appreciate the help and support of a peer, and nurturers feel gratified and satisfied.

You may think this would be most valuable if the buddy is one who is bilingual in English and the beginner's native language, or at least one at a more advanced level of English language development. While this type of pairing can be highly beneficial, it may also be fraught with risk by encouraging overtranslation of concepts and information from the readings. It may place an undue burden on the buddy and lead to the beginner's dependence on the translation and the translator. It can sometimes even slow down the language learner's development of English reading skills. In reality, any willing student can offer enough help and support to make a difference.

Buddies can work together to use some of the strategies presented in earlier sections of this chapter. Review, for example, some of the less linguistically demanding textbook aids. With a little help, the beginner could focus on getting information from charts, tables, diagrams, maps, pictures, and other illustrations. Buddies can also help with vocabulary. They can assist beginners in the language detective activity, in locating and explaining synonyms and idioms, and in encouraging generous use of personal and bilingual dictionaries.

## Alternative Textbooks

Another approach for students at beginning levels of English language development is to supplement your regular classroom textbook with one that is written either at a lower reading level or in the students' native language. While this strategy may offer a small short-term advantage, it has a greater number of both short- and long-term disadvantages.

Using an alternative textbook is stigmatizing, especially one written at a lower level. It sends a subtle, unintended message that those who use it are less capable than the others in the class. Using a native language textbook may violate state laws concerning the use of a language other than English in the classroom. Even if no legal issues are involved, students using native language textbooks may become dependent on them to the point of not wanting to make any attempts at using the regular classroom text. Much like using a translator, it may impede the development of English language skills.

The use of native language textbooks presents an additional difficulty. Your beginning English language students may be from several language backgrounds. It is improbable that you could find suitable textbooks in each of the languages spoken by the beginners in your classroom And if you can't find native language textbooks for all, is it fair to find texts for only some?

There is no magic formula to help the true English language beginners in your content class. These strategies are probably the best you can use for a while because, at the very least, they allow the student to learn some content and they show that you care.

## CHOOSING A TEXTBOOK

You may be fortunate enough to be asked to choose a textbook from several available possibilities. Or you may find yourself in the enviable position of being on the school or district selection committee for new textbooks. You may even be asked to give input on new state adoptions. These guidelines can help you make informed decisions.

The guidelines presented here are designed with the English language learner in mind. They will help you choose textbooks that maximize the potential for these students' academic success. However, these guidelines really have a much wider application. All students, of all subjects, and in all grades will enjoy textbooks that exhibit the same characteristics and qualities that are so helpful to English language learners.

### Content: First and Foremost

No amount of "book appeal" can replace content that is inadequate to meet your curriculum requirements or your state standards. So in big letters at the top of the list of guidelines is CONTENT. And the key question is this: *Is the content a good fit with your curriculum and state standards?* If your response to that question is positive, then your review can move ahead with these additional questions.

- Is the content current and accurate?
- Are the topics presented in a developmentally logical manner?
- Are new concepts supported with appropriate amounts of background information and review?
- Are topics explained in a clear and concise manner?
- Are topics covered in appropriate depth?
- Do questions and/or suggested activities develop critical thinking and problem-solving skills?
- Is new or technical vocabulary clearly defined when it is introduced?
- Are ethnic and cultural diversity issues represented to an adequate degree?

When you've determined that the textbook content works well with your curriculum, then it is time to consider several other factors.

## Considerate Text

*Considerate text* is a term applied to textbooks that support students' learning by using vocabulary and language structure appropriate to their experience and ability. Considerate texts enhance students' comprehension through appropriate selection and use of language, informational cohesion and unity, readability level, and organization. Considerate text makes content-area textbooks user-friendly, more enjoyable to read, and easier to understand. Figure 5.19 presents a textbook page that illustrates the concept of considerate text.

A simple way to evaluate the type of language used in a textbook is to analyze several sentences selected at random. As you read each sentence, pay attention to the level and diversity of vocabulary, and to length and structural complexity of the sentence itself.

To evaluate text cohesion and unity, try this: Choose a chapter and read *only* the chapter title, then each heading followed by the first sentence of that section. In texts with a high degree of informational unity and cohesion, you will be able to see a logical progression of information, sufficient to give you at least a general understanding of the topic.

Readability levels are determined by complicated formulae and are best left to experts. The readability level of a textbook should be available to you through the text's publisher.

Finally, organization of the text is a loosely defined category that is made up of a number of elements. They are discussed in the additional guidelines that follow.

## First Impressions Really Count!

Have you ever had the experience of opening a textbook for a course that you were about to begin and thinking, "Uh oh, this course is going to be really hard!" What you're reacting to is not the difficulty of the course, but the *perceived* difficulty of the textbook, and that perception is based largely on how the book looks. We really *do* judge a book by its cover—or at least by the cover and a quick flip through the pages! First impressions often shape our long-range views. Your students' attitudes to the whole course can be positively or negatively affected by their initial reactions toward their textbooks.

Students react initially to the organization and design of a textbook. What determines whether students *think* the subject matter is learnable or not doesn't relate at all to the actual content. Students judge a textbook first by its overall appearance—organization and layout of sections, chapters, and pages—and by the type, variety, and frequency of textbook aids.

**Atoms**

In order to understand the makeup of matter, you need to know more about atoms. Atoms are the smallest particles of an element. Atoms can exist alone or in combination. They are too small to be seen without a special microscope. If you could see atoms, they would look like tiny planets with moons circling around them.

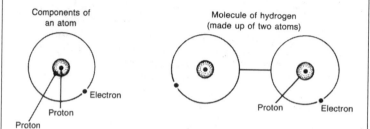

The diagram shows an oversimplified structure of an atom and a molecule of hydrogen with two atoms.

Atoms are made up of **neutrons**, **protons**, and **electrons**. Neutrons are particles of matter that contain no **electrical charge**. Protons are particles of matter that contain a positive (+) electrical charge. Protons and neutrons stick together in the center of the atom. The tiny moons that move around the **nucleus**, or center of the atom, are called electrons. They have very little mass compared to the heavier protons and neutrons. The electrons have a negative (−) electrical charge. They are attracted to the positive charge of the protons. The attraction is strong enough to pull the electrons toward the center. The high speed of the electrons keeps them in a kind of **orbit**, or circular path, around the protons and neutrons.

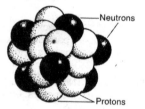

Protons and neutrons sticking together in the center of the atom

**FIGURE 5.19. An Example of Considerate Text (From M. A. Christison and S. Bassano, *Earth and Physical Science: Content and Learning Strategies* Teacher's Edition, Addison-Wesley, 1992, p.79)**

## Layout

The textbook layout determines its overall attractiveness. For textbooks with "student appeal," focus on these individual elements:

1. Length of chapters and section subdivisions
   - Shorter is better. Information that is broken up into smaller chunks feels more learnable.

2. Size and style of the typeface
   - Larger type and more space between lines of print make a text easier to read.

3. Amount of white space on the page
   - Wider margins and more space between sections make content look more readily comprehensible.

4. Paper quality and color
   - Glossy white paper makes print easier to read than paper that is ivory colored and has a matte finish.

5. Amount and variety of graphic design features
   - An interesting *cover* invites the reader to open the book.
   - *Illustrations* embed context and make the text more comprehensible. Look for charts, maps, graphs, diagrams, and tables that are colorful, interesting, relevant, and varied.
   - *Pictures* and *photographs* enhance text. They should be modern looking, topically appropriate, and culturally diverse.
   - *Organizers* and *highlighters* emphasize and clarify teaching points and key concepts. Look for generous use of boxes, bullets, bolding, and color.
   - *Balance of graphics to text* should be appropriate. Pages should not appear dense or cluttered.

## Textbook Aids

Textbook aids form a system of support to facilitate students' understanding of the printed material. Textbooks vary widely in their use of special aids to comprehension, not only in how many they include, but also in type, clarity, and format.

While all students gain from using textbook aids, English language learners, in particular, often depend upon them. Examine textbook choices with these factors in mind:

- *Contents*: Is it specific enough to locate categories of information?
- *Index*: How inclusive is it?

- *Glossary*: Is there one? If so, how are the words highlighted in the text? How clear are the definitions of words in the glossary?
- *Appendixes*: Are there any? Do they contain supplementary information that extends interest and/or enriches topics?
- *Chapter openers*: Is there an overview, outline, or question section at the beginning of each chapter to give focus to what will follow?
- *Summaries*: Is information summarized at the ends of subsections and at the end of each chapter?
- *Chapter closers*: Are there review questions and topics to think about that promote critical thinking and discussion at the end of each chapter?

Textbook aids of special value to English language learners also include some of the items listed in the layout section. Charts, maps, photos, pictures, diagrams, graphs, and tables visually contextualize print. Words in boldfaced type call attention to key concepts and important words and phrases. Boxes and bulleted or numbered lists highlight important information. These linguistically simplified elements serve as aids to students by embedding context and facilitating comprehension.

## One Last Question

There is probably no textbook that is absolutely perfect for your class, but some will come much closer to your ideal than others. After you have used these guidelines and completed a thorough examination of your choices, one final question remains: Ask yourself, *Is this a textbook **I** would like to use?*

# CHAPTER 6

# Strategies to Modify Assignments

---

**Case Study—Back to Mr. Elkind's Classroom**

Mr. Elkind, the middle school social studies teacher, enjoys seeing his students actively involved in their own learning. His classroom is a dynamic place, filled with daily activities designed to develop and enrich his students' understanding of the topics they're studying.

For every unit, he creates exciting and unusual ideas for projects and encourages his students to choose the ones that interest them—anything from reading historical novels to doing specialized research on the Internet. His homework assignments build background for lessons or reinforce what was learned in class. Most of the students love his class because he makes history come alive.

---

Wonderful? Yes, but think for a moment about the language demand of these activities. Mr. Elkind's assignments and projects involve a heavy load of reading, research, and writing. For the English language learners in his class, history is more frustrating than lively.

What kind of assignments can Mr. Elkind create for his ELLs that maintain a high level of cognitive challenge while reducing the linguistic load? He and other content teachers need to look beyond the traditional techniques of question-and-answer, research reports, and oral presentations to strategies that engage ELL students in alternative means and products. The goal is to build rich conceptual understanding of content while keeping the language input and output as simple as possible.

The strategies presented in this chapter are of two types: strategies that present ideas to modify the regular assignments you use with the whole class, and then, strategies that offer ideas for alternative but parallel activities.

## MODIFYING WHOLE CLASS ASSIGNMENTS

Strategies that reduce the language demand will make your regular assignments more accessible to the English language learners in your classes. These modifications are widely adaptable with many types of homework and in-class activities.

### Offer a Word Bank

For assignments that require simple, short answers to a series of questions, consider using a word bank. Word banks are lists of content-related word or phrase choices. Students select items from the list to correctly answer the assigned questions. Including a number of extra word or phrase choices that relate closely to the topic will raise the level of challenge and promote critical thinking.

Word banks work well with many straightforward questions that check comprehension after textbook readings. They are also well suited to assignments that ask students to label, for example, parts of a diagram in science or specific items on maps in social studies. They can be used as an additional support in combination with many of the strategies discussed below. Word banks allow ELLs to focus their attention on content by lowering the language demand.

### Assign Fewer Questions

Textbook readings usually have a set of questions at the end of the chapter to check comprehension and to encourage students to think critically about the topic. An assignment that seems reasonable for your native-speaking students may feel overwhelming to your English language learners. They will be able to respond better if you assign fewer questions, focusing on those that are either more conceptually important or less linguistically complex.

Textbook comprehension questions are written to check students' understanding of broad concepts as well as specific facts. Some questions are conceptually more central to the topic than others. By assigning only the more important questions, your language learners can focus their efforts on those that are most critical to their understanding.

The second way to approach the strategy of assigning fewer questions is to select those that are linguistically easier to complete. Questions vary in the amount and type of information required to answer them. Some questions can be adequately answered with a single word or short phrase while others require much longer, more linguistically complex responses. Consider assigning language learners written responses to only those questions that are linguistically simple to answer, and use an alternative assignment (strategies of this type appear in the next section of this chapter) for questions requiring a longer, more complicated written answer.

## Allot Extra Time

English language learners need more time to get their work done. In effect, they are doing a double assignment: They must first decode the language and then deliver the content. With this extra burden in mind, allow additional time for ELLs to complete readings and assignments.

## Evaluate for Content Only

While you probably require the use of good grammar and complete sentences as a normal part of your regular assignments, try to remember that if your English language learners could write that way, they wouldn't be classified as ESOL. So, for them, evaluate their assignments for accuracy of content information only. Look for key content words or phrases that signify some grasp of the topic under study and give credit for those. Accept grammar and spelling errors as long as the content is correct. Think about the *message* they're sending, not about the *means* through which it is being sent.

## Offer Models and Outlines

Many written assignments follow a relatively standardized type of paragraph structure. For these, consider giving the English language learners a model, an outline, or a preformatted page to follow. This strategy also appeals to native-speaking students who find written work, in general, a challenge. Students, native speakers and language learners alike, often feel more able to tackle an assignment when they don't have to begin by facing a completely blank page.

Think about the kinds of written assignments you give. Most assignments ask students to classify, identify, list, explain, describe, predict, and compare and contrast, in words much like those listed in Figure 6.1. Student responses follow a basic pattern that can be modeled to lighten the linguistic burden. Figures 6.2 and 6.3 illustrate response models for questions in science and social studies, respectively.

Many types of written assignments lend themselves to modeled formatting. In science classes, for example, students often are required to write up experiments, demonstrations, or activities done in class. Figure 6.4 shows a format that students can use for this purpose. Structuring the language and pattern of these reports lets English language learners concentrate on the cognitive processing of what they are learning instead of having to focus on creating language for the response. In addition, repeated exposure to formatted patterns teaches ELLs how to formulate appropriate responses when this scaffolding strategy is removed.

Modifications in regular assignments can be tremendously helpful for English language learners. Even small changes, like the inclusion of a word bank, can mean the difference between feelings of frustration and feelings of success.

- Describe the process by which _____ causes _____.
- Describe the factors that affect _____.
- Describe the characteristics of _____.
- Describe how _____ (changes/uses) _____.
- Describe conditions that cause _____.
- Describe how _____ form.
- Name and describe (two) kinds of _____.
- List factors that affect _____.
- List and explain the main types of _____.
- Identify and explain the effects of _____.
- Explain why _____ is important to _____.
- Give examples of how _____ uses _____.

**FIGURE 6.1. Typical Writing Assignments That Can Be Modeled**

**Earth Science Comprehension Question:** Name and define the three major types of interactions among organisms.

**Modeled Response: Three Types of Interactions Among Organisms**

The first type of interaction is called _____. This means

_____.

The second type of interaction is called _____. This means

_____.

The third type of interaction is called _____. This means

_____.

**FIGURE 6.2. Modeled Responses to Comprehension Questions in Science**

**American History Comprehension Question:** What was the goal of the Open Door Policy in China? Did it succeed?

**Modeled Response**

The goal of the Open Door Policy in China was to _____.

_____ It (was/was not)

successful because _____

_____.

FIGURE 6.3. Modeled Responses to Comprehension Questions in Social Studies

**Name of Experiment:** _____

We wanted to show that _____

_____ .

We used (materials) _____ , _____ , _____ ,

_____ , _____ , _____ .

The first thing we did was _____

_____ .

The second thing we did was _____

_____ .

The third thing we did was _____

_____ .

What happened was _____

_____ .

This happened because _____

_____ .

This shows that _____

_____ .

FIGURE 6.4. Model for Write-up of Science Demonstration

Try to look at assignments as your English language learners might see them. Anticipating areas of language difficulty and making appropriate modifications will go a long way to helping your language learners demonstrate their comprehension of the content you teach.

## DEVELOPING ALTERNATIVE ASSIGNMENTS

The second type of strategy to modify written work involves developing parallel or alternative assignments for your English language learners. The goal of these assignments is to create engaging activities that maintain a high level of cognitive challenge and, at the same time, lower language demand. Your small investment of time and effort to put these ideas to work in your classroom will yield big returns for you and your students.

### Diagrams, Maps, and Charts

Students are often required to engage in factual, descriptive content writing. English language learners can convey much of the same information alternatively through graphic or visual means. ELLs can complete a diagram, map, chart, or drawing instead. They can supplement names and labels with related descriptive words or explanatory phrases. Students can expand the drawings of the eye shown in Figure 6.5, for example, to include additional functional or descriptive data. On other types of diagrams, students can classify items by color-coding or indicate relationships among elements by adding arrows. Figure 6.6 uses separate drawings to label and explain a type of ocean movement.

### Sequenced Pictures

English language learners can show their understanding by drawing or arranging a set of pictures. While other students are completing an assignment in standard paragraph form, language learners can be doing the same assignment through graphics. Figure 6.7 shows the process and results of an in-class science experiment as a series of sequenced pictures. The student who did these drawings demonstrated a clear understanding of the experiment in a way that would have been impossible in a written report.

Sequenced pictures can depict steps or stages, or they can be as simple as *before* and *after*. After the pictures have been drawn or arranged, students can supplement the pictures with additional appropriate information. Students whose English language skills are at the beginner stage can label parts of each picture—you can even offer them a word bank. Students at higher levels can add descriptive and explanatory words, phrases, and sentences.

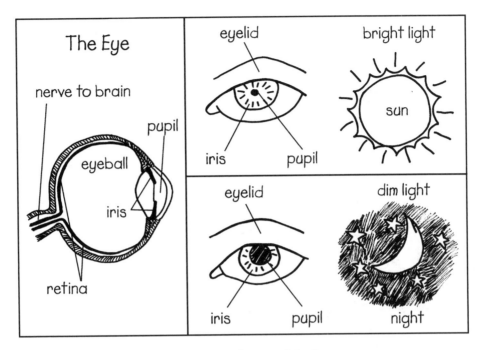

**FIGURE 6.5. Diagram of the Eye**

## Graphic Organizers

It is likely that you make frequent use of graphic organizers as a routine part of your teaching. Have you ever thought of using them as alternative assignments for English language learners?

Graphic organizers are interesting and easy for English language learners to work with. Some graphic organizers are widely adaptable, while others are more tightly structured. It is important to predetermine the most appropriate graphic format to convey the information that your other students will be expressing in written form.

### The Cluster or Web

The graphic organizer with the widest application and greatest flexibility uses the concept of clustering or webbing as shown in Figure 6.8. Students are able to give a maximum amount of information with only a minimum amount of language. Cluster or web organizers are useful for explaining topics with multiple elements and for showing relationships among the elements. This type of organizer would work well in social studies, for example, to show causes of World War II or factors influencing immigration to the United States in the early 1900s. In science, a cluster or web would be appropriate to categorize, classify, and describe types and subtypes of substances and structures.

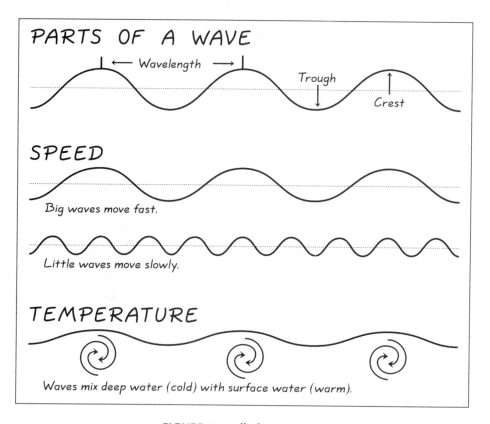

**FIGURE 6.6. All About Waves**

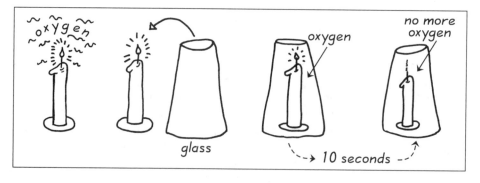

**FIGURE 6.7. Sequenced Pictures of a Science Experiment**

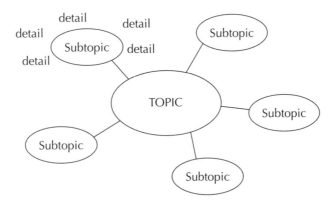

**FIGURE 6.8. The Cluster or Web**

## *The Problem-Solving Organizer*

A more tightly controlled form of clustering is the problem-solving organizer, shown in Figure 6.9. It is a concept map designed to show multiple and sequential cause and effect. It can be effectively used when more direct relationships and linear patterns need to be explained.

The problem-solving organizer is structured around a central issue or problem. It visually depicts causes of the issue or problem, actions taken to deal with the issue or problem, and results or effects of these actions. Language learners can use this organizer in science and social studies classes as an alternative to written reports on environmental and societal issues, such as those listed in Figure 6.10. The problem-solving organizer is an ideal way for students to express complex ideas and relationships in a linguistically simplified manner.

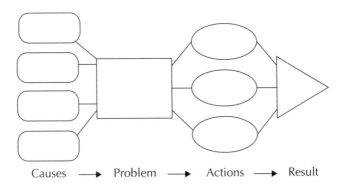

**FIGURE 6.9. The Problem-Solving Organizer**

| Environmental Issues | Societal Issues |
| --- | --- |
| Global Warming | Slavery |
| Air or Water Pollution | Reconstruction of Post–Civil War South |
| Recycling | Rise of Labor Unions |
| Endangered Species | The Cold War |
| Depletion of Tropical Rain Forests | Terrorism |

**FIGURE 6.10. Topics for Using Problem-Solving Organizers in Science and Social Studies**

## Venn Diagrams

Venn diagrams are familiar to most teachers and students. They are used to show similarities and differences among concepts, events, people, or things. Figure 6.11 illustrates the Venn diagram in its most common form, comparing and contrasting two elements. However, students may also enjoy the challenge of comparing *three* things, as in Figure 6.12. Like other graphic organizers, Venn diagrams reduce language demand to single words and phrases and allow English language learners to focus on the content.

## Time Lines

Time lines graphically show chronological sequences and temporal relationships. Time lines can be drawn to record developments over periods as short as seconds or as long as many millennia. They can, for example, illustrate chemical change of matter within seconds or minutes, depict historical development over a single century, or show the evolution of man over hundreds of thousands of years. The time line in Figure 6.13 shows when the various departments in the

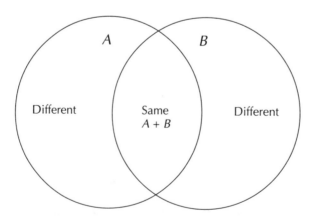

**FIGURE 6.11. Venn Diagram Comparing Two Things**

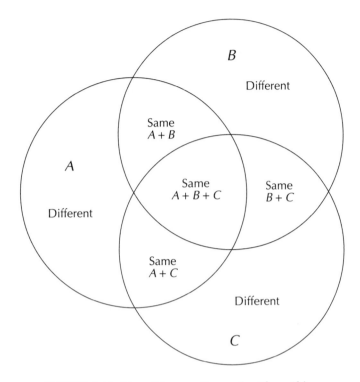

**FIGURE 6.12. Venn Diagram Comparing Three Things**

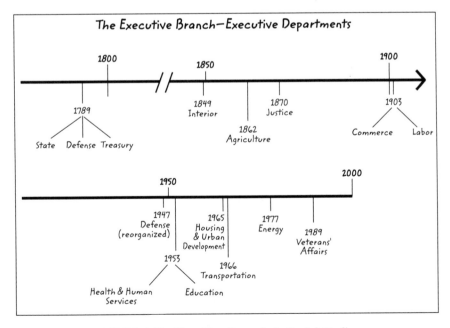

**FIGURE 6.13. Time Line Example in Social Studies**

executive branch of government were created. Students can write in additional information to explain the function and focus of each department.

Students can draw *parallel time lines* to compare two or more chains of related activity over simultaneous time periods, as in a time line representing developments in land, sea, and air transportation from 1800 to 2000. Or students can expand a segment of a time line to add greater detail to a short period within the longer time line. Time lines are readily adaptable and simple to create. They convey a great deal of information in very few words—a good combination of qualities for language-learning students.

### The Matrix

The matrix, as shown in Figure 6.14, is a form of attribute charting. The matrix is a grid that visually compares the key variables of a set of related items. Figure 6.15 shows a matrix for science that compares the characteristics and qualities of five different mineral substances. In social studies, the matrix is useful to compare qualities and achievements of selected presidents or geographic and economic features of several countries or regions.

Matrix grids can give information about variables in a number of different ways. Students can fill boxes with a plus or minus sign to denote the presence or absence of something or insert a number to specify an exact amount or percentage. They can write in descriptive words or short phrases, or give specific representative names.

The matrix is a graphic organizer that is versatile and widely adaptable. Its use as an alternative assignment allows English language learners to convey important content information in a linguistically simplified manner.

| Qualities →<br>Items to Compare ↓ | 1 | 2 | 3 | 4 | 5 |
|---|---|---|---|---|---|
| A | | | | | |
| B | | | | | |
| C | | | | | |
| D | | | | | |
| E | | | | | |

**FIGURE 6.14. The Matrix**

| Specimen | Luster | Cleavage | Hardness | Color | Other |
|----------|--------|----------|----------|-------|-------|
| A |  |  |  |  |  |
| B |  |  |  |  |  |
| C |  |  |  |  |  |
| D |  |  |  |  |  |
| E |  |  |  |  |  |

**FIGURE 6.15. The Matrix in Science: Comparing Minerals**

## Hands-On Assignments

Manipulatives and other hands-on learning materials offer another option for English language learners to demonstrate their understanding of complex or abstract concepts in a concrete, visual manner. ELLs, especially at the beginners' level, can show conceptual understanding through dioramas or models, or by presenting an appropriate experiment, exhibit, or demonstration.

## THE NEXT STEP: BUILDING LANGUAGE

Graphic organizers and other alternative assignments are productive means for English language learners to show what they know. However, if they are required to do only this type of written assignment, they will make slow progress in developing their English language and literacy skills. Language learners, at a developmentally appropriate point, need to move from relying on graphics to building language.

An effective way to help students develop English literacy skills is to develop models, outlines, or formatted sentences to take them from graphics to the next step. All graphic organizers can be formatted to build language. Figure 6.16 presents examples of formatted models that students can use to convert information from their time lines to complete sentences. Figure 6.17 does the same for Venn diagrams. Although the complexity of the problem-solving organizer requires a bit more ingenuity to create a simple format, Figure 6.18 shows a generic model that teachers can modify to fit specific topics. Additionally, consider using the T-notes discussed in Chapter 5, Figure 5.14, or the formatted models or outlines discussed earlier in this chapter in the section on modifying whole class assignments.

The types of assignments you choose for your English language learners will depend on the combination of the content itself and the students' level of

**Model 1**

In _____, _____ occurred.
      year       event

          _____ was invented by _____.
          product

          _____ was born.
          person

          _____ gained independence.
          country

**Model 2**

_____ began in _____ and ended in _____.
    Event           year           year

_____ began in the _____
  Trend or movement           ordinal number (first/third/middle)

_____ of the _____.
  period (decade/quarter/half)       ___ century

**FIGURE 6.16. Using Time Lines to Build Language**

When we compare _____ to _____, we can see that some things are the same and some things are different.

The things that are the same are _____

_____

_____.

The things that are different are _____

_____

_____.

**FIGURE 6.17. Using Venn Diagrams to Build Language**

The issue (problem) of _____ has (several, four,

many) causes. The causes are _____

_____.

People (agencies, the government) have tried to deal with this issue

(problem) by _____

_____

_____.

These actions have (helped, not helped) because _____

_____.

The issue (problem) of _____ (has been resolved, needs

more action, is unchanged, is growing, etc.).

**FIGURE 6.18. Using the Problem-Solving Organizer to Build Language**

language development. Students need to start with simple tasks and move on to more complex ones. Remember that CALP, or academic language, develops slowly over a long period of time.

During the developmental process, you can maximize content learning for ELLs by making assignments context-embedded—that is, moving them from Cummins's Quadrant IV to Quadrant III (Figure 2.1 in Chapter 2). Alternative and modified assignments allow students to demonstrate their understanding of content while they are building language skills. These assignments balance high levels of cognitive challenge with low levels of language demand so that language learners can begin to experience academic success.

# CHAPTER 7

# Adapting Techniques of Classroom Instruction

Students learn because teachers teach—a simple truth. It is also true that students learn better when they have good teachers. A good teacher facilitates comprehension by making learning interesting and "learnable."

What do you need to know to be a good teacher to the English language learners in your classroom? How can you make your classroom instruction more accessible to them?

The four groups of strategies in this chapter—activating background knowledge, clarifying comprehension, increasing teacher-student interaction, and increasing student-student interaction—are more than just good teaching techniques. For English language learners they form the foundation for comprehensible instruction. Incorporating these strategies into your regular classroom instruction offers your students a better chance to succeed in learning the content you are teaching.

## WHY IS BACKGROUND KNOWLEDGE SO IMPORTANT?

Background knowledge is fundamental to new learning. It has been said that the single best indicator of how well a student can learn new content is the amount of relevant background knowledge or experience he or she already has. That's why activating students' prior knowledge is an essential teaching strategy.

A student's own background knowledge forms the building blocks upon which new learning is built. Activating that background knowledge makes learning meaningful, awakens interest in the topic, and increases motivation. All students, not only language-learning students, benefit from making explicit connections between past and present learning. So why is this a special issue for English language learners?

School curriculum is planned around a set of basic assumptions about common academic background and life experience of students at each grade level. Students coming from other countries, however, have generally had differing sets of personal, cultural, and academic experiences. For the English language learners in their classes, teachers must first determine that they actually have the relevant background to be successful in learning the new content. The second step is then to *build* background knowledge where it is lacking before presenting the new material.

What students already know virtually determines how well they will learn new content. The strategies presented in this section will simultaneously activate prior knowledge for students who have it and build new knowledge for those who need it.

## STRATEGIES TO ACTIVATE BACKGROUND KNOWLEDGE

### Brainstorm

Brainstorming is a simple and effective strategy to introduce a new topic. It activates students' background knowledge and engages their interest. At the same time, the teacher can determine whether or not students have enough background knowledge to move ahead.

To begin brainstorming, write a topic word on the board or on an overhead transparency. Accompany it with the open-ended question, *"What do you think of when I say the word _____?"*

As students respond, write their words and phrases around the topic word to form a graphic display. Accept all answers, right or wrong. When you feel ready to move on with the lesson, tell students that you will return later to re-examine these ideas by saying something like, *"Let's save these answers. We'll come back to them later to see what we found out about them."*

A variation of this strategy is called carousel brainstorming, explained in Figure 7.1. This technique has the additional benefit of getting students up and

---

Tape sheets of chart paper on the walls at various locations around your classroom. At the top of each sheet, write a word or phrase pertaining to the new topic to be studied. For large groups and to save time, have several sets of the same words or phrases.

Following your signals, students walk around the room in small groups writing their associations to the word at the top of each paper. Allow no more than two minutes before signaling time to move to the next location.

**FIGURE 7.1. Carousel Brainstorming**

physically moving, involving all students simultaneously. It is exciting to watch students' faces as they come up with new ideas triggered by reading what other students have written. At the end of the activity, groups can read out items from each sheet of chart paper as you create a single brainstorming graphic based on all the information written.

At the end of the lesson, return to the display and use it to summarize and review. As you point to a specific word or phrase and ask, *"Did we talk about this?"*, students can review what they learned in the lesson. They can add new words and phrases and correct misconceptions. You can make connections to subtopics to be covered in later lessons.

Students can copy the graphic on a piece of paper to serve as a study guide. If you do the brainstorming activity on an overhead transparency or on chart paper, you can use it again at the start of the next day's lesson to review previous learning. Brainstorming is a particularly easy and advantageous way of activating or building prior knowledge.

## Think-Pair-Share

Think-Pair-Share is a technique that activates prior knowledge and, at the same time, encourages participation. Start with the same open-ended question as in the brainstorming activity, but this time, instead of asking the class for an immediate oral response, give students one or two minutes to jot down any related words or phrases they can *think* of. Then, for the next minute or two, *pair* students up with a partner to discuss and expand their individual lists. Finally, invite students to *share* their ideas with the rest of the class. A great way to do this is to ask students to tell you an idea they either *had* or *heard*. This technique actively supports learning, gets the students immediately involved in the topic, and guarantees more participation.

## Use a K-W-L-H Chart

A graphic organizer that complements the Think-Pair-Share activity is the K-W-L-H chart (Figure 7.2). Students are asked to write what they already <u>k</u>now (or think they know) about a topic in the **K** column. They then discuss what they <u>w</u>ant to know with a partner or in a small group to complete the **W** column. They complete the **L** and **H** columns at the end of the lesson by listing what they <u>l</u>earned and <u>h</u>ow they learned it. The **H** column is optional; however, it is an effective way of focusing awareness on learning strategies. Making daily entries in each column as topical information builds forms an ongoing means of activating students' prior knowledge and stimulating critical thinking.

Working in pairs or small groups to fill in the **W** and **L** sections is important for English language learners. ELLs lack the specific vocabulary needed to complete these parts, especially at the introductory stage of a topic, which is when this strategy is most frequently used. For ELLs and other students who

| What do I know? | What do I want to know? | What have I learned? | How did I learn it? |
|---|---|---|---|
|  |  |  |  |

**FIGURE 7.2. K-W-L-H Chart**

may be unfamiliar with a topic, the task may, at first, seem impossible. Without the give-and-take of some discussion, native and nonnative students alike often sit staring at blank columns. How can they know what they *want* to know when they don't even know anything about this topic in the first place? Talking about the topic helps students generate ideas.

## Personalize the Lesson

Asking students to talk about their own experiences as they relate to new content is an excellent way to activate and build background knowledge. It stimulates students' initial interest in the topic and demonstrates its relatedness to the real world.

An introduction to a unit on the Civil War, for example, often includes a discussion of how differences among individuals and groups can lead to conflict. Students who have lived outside the United States may have first-hand knowledge of conflicts based on political, ethnic, or religious differences in their native countries. On a more personal level, some students, including the native English-speakers, may want to share stories about "family feuds." In science, students may have first-hand knowledge of unusual types of terrain or weather. Can any of your students talk about living in or near rain forests, mountains, deserts, oceans, or rivers, or experiencing a tornado, hurricane, or earthquake? Some may have lived in or near areas with visible air or water pollution. Sharing this type of knowledge awakens immediate personal interest and allows you to draw comparisons and make generalizations.

Students—all students—enjoy sharing individual experiences. It's an attention-getting way to begin a new topic.

## Linking Lessons

Every lesson benefits from linking new concepts to students' past learning and experience. Start daily lessons with openers that activate knowledge from previous lessons on the same topic. Making explicit connections between concepts serves as a form of reinforcement and review. By regularly stimulating background knowledge, you facilitate students' continuing conceptual development and increase the potential for new learning and enhanced retention.

## CLARIFYING COMPREHENSION

### Check Comprehension

It is every teacher's greatest desire that students *really* understand the content that has just been taught. Teachers want to be able to clarify, repeat, explain, and correct any misunderstandings before moving ahead. So, several times during the lesson, they check student comprehension with questions that sound something like these:

> Does everyone understand?
>
> Does anyone have any questions?
>
> Does anyone need me to repeat anything?
>
> OK, so everybody gets it?

The response to these questions is usually profound silence, even when students have no idea of what was just taught. Why? Because these kinds of questions ask a student to raise a hand and publicly identify him- or herself as *the only one* in the whole class who just didn't get it. Who would ever want to do a thing like that? Better to just sit there and *feel* dumb than to raise your hand and have everyone *know* how dumb you really are!

The unintended effect of these questions is exactly the opposite of the teacher's sincere objective. How, then, can you word a question that will actually achieve your desired goal? Try this:

> It's question time. Who's got a question for me?

These words make it sound like questions are a normal and expected part of every lesson.

You can reinforce your accepting attitude toward questions even further when you respond to a student's question with something very positive:

> That's a great question!
>
> Thank you for asking that!
>
> Good question!

Responses like these actually make students feel *rewarded* for asking for clarification, instead of penalized by drawing negative attention to themselves.

Try it! You'll see the change immediately when you say, "Question time. Who's got a question for me?", instead of the traditional, "Does everyone understand?" *You* will be rewarded by your students' response.

## Give Clear Directions

Have you ever been a student in a class where you've been given directions that you didn't understand? You sat there with a growing sense of anxiety because you had absolutely no idea of what to do. You looked around—had others already started working? Are you the only one who didn't get it? Perhaps you quietly asked several of your peers if they knew what you were supposed to do, only to discover that they didn't know either. By now you are all feeling considerably less capable than you felt just a few minutes ago. Anxiety is never a good way to begin an assignment.

Successful activities begin with good directions. Here is a simple, five-step plan to assure that your instructions will be clearly understood by all your students. These steps are summarized in Figure 5.3.

1. *Say* the directions. Explain them as explicitly as you possibly can. State what you want students to do in a simple, step-by-step manner. If the directions are complex, use the "one-step" approach: Tell students that after they complete the first step, you'll tell them what to do next.
2. *Write* them on the board, on chart paper, or on an overhead transparency. Written words reinforce spoken language and help language learners process what they are being asked to do. Keep the written directions on view so students can refer to them as needed during the assignment.
3. *Model* the process and the product. Demonstrate how to begin, and explain the choices you make to reach the final product. Show students what a finished product should look like. Show possible variations. Adding this visual element to your directions is vital for your ELLs because it shortcuts your need for wordy explanation. It also gives all students a clear understanding of your expectations.
4. *Check comprehension* by asking the students to repeat, step by step, what they are expected to do. Start by asking, "So, what's the first thing we're going to do?" Go through each step of the activity, adding detail or correcting as needed. It is important for the students themselves to explain each of the steps they are going to take to complete the project. After all, they are the ones who will be doing the activity.
5. *Ask for questions*—"Question time. Who's got a question for me?" Most likely they'll have none.

Clear directions start students out right. Students can focus immediately and confidently on the work to be done—no wasted time, no wasted anxiety. Good instructions give students the best chance of producing a satisfying result.

**1.** Say the directions clearly.

**2.** Write them and leave them on view.

**3.** Model the process and the product.

**4.** Check comprehension.

**5.** Ask for questions.

**FIGURE 7.3. Five Steps to Giving Clear Directions**

## Create Homework Routines

Teachers often run out of time at the end of the lesson. The homework assignment, usually the last piece of information in the class, often gets delivered in a hurried rush of words as students are packing up their books and getting ready to leave. For English language learners, this can be a confusing and difficult situation.

Try instead to write homework assignments ahead of time in the same place everyday. The place you choose can be a small section of the board, on chart paper, or on an overhead transparency. If you don't want your students to see the assignment at the beginning of class because they may be tempted to work on it during class time, keep it covered until an appropriate point in the lesson. The main objective is to avoid rushing it out orally as the bell is ringing. Make sure students know that homework information will appear in the same place every day. Your students can never use the excuse that they didn't hear you.

## Allow Extra Time

Plan to give your English language learners extra time to practice and apply new concepts. Assignments and activities can easily take twice the amount of time for ELLs because of their need to attend to the language as well as the content requirements. Remember that they are learning English at the same time that they are learning *in* English.

## End Each Lesson with Review

Teachers, with the objective of maximizing the use of every minute of class time for learning, often run out of time at the end of class to conduct a review. With all good intentions, those who do this discard a critically important teaching strategy.

All students, and ELLs in particular, benefit from spending the last three minutes of class time in review. Every lesson needs closure, even those that will be continued the next day. Just before class ends, either return to the brainstorming graphic for review or ask the simple question, "So, what did we cover today?" If important information is omitted, make your question more specific, as in "What about _____? What did we learn about that?"

Review is the cement that holds the learning together. It reinforces learning and makes it more solid. Students get to hear information that may have been originally unclear. You get feedback and the opportunity to correct any misconceptions. The value of routine review and summary of information covered during the class period far exceeds the short time devoted to it.

## INCREASING TEACHER-STUDENT INTERACTION IN THE CLASSROOM

Students thrive in classrooms where teachers promote learning through participation and interaction. Do you interact with *all* the students in your classroom?

### Monitor Your Interaction Patterns

An interesting way to systematically monitor your interaction with students is to videotape a class you teach. As you watch the taped lesson, observe your patterns of interaction. You may make some unexpected discoveries.

Many teachers are amazed to find that they have a distinct *action zone*, that is, a localized area of the classroom that they favor. This is the zone of students toward which they direct their lessons. Unconsciously, they look at and call on the students in this section much more than the others.

Watching your videotape will help you determine whether you favor a particular section of the classroom during teaching presentations and discussions. Use a class-seating chart to carefully note where you stand and who you look at as you teach. Note which students you call on and how many times. Your tallies may make you aware of an action zone you never knew you had.

Teachers have made other interesting discoveries from viewing themselves teaching. Some were surprised that they had called on several of their students so many times. Others saw that they had neglected to call on several very quiet students in the class, even though they were positive that they had actively involved every single student. Still others realized that they might improve student participation by working on smiling more and moving around the room.

If you videotape yourself teaching and you like what you see, give yourself a pat on the back. If, on the other hand, you feel you need to find ways to increase opportunities for your students to participate, there are several techniques you might try. A simple strategy that teachers use is to check off students' names on a class list or seating chart. Another idea is to write students' names on popsicle sticks, place the sticks name-side down in a cup, and randomly draw one after asking a question. (Use your teacher prerogative if you think the question may be too difficult for the name you draw by saying "Oops, I just called this name," or "Absent.") One teacher instituted a rule that all students who didn't participate had to conduct the review at the end of the class. It was amazing how the participation in this class increased!

## Encourage Participation

Encouraging participation involves more than just calling on all the students in your class. To encourage the participation of your ELL students, start by making friendly eye contact and smiling at each of them. Then consider ways to lower both the language difficulty of your questions and the anxiety of answering them.

### Try a Whole Class Response Technique

A good strategy to involve all students at the same time is to use a whole class response technique, but not an oral one—not the traditional choral response in which the teacher never really knows who is answering and who is not. There are several better ideas to get all the students responding simultaneously to your questions.

1. Students make the *Thumbs Up/Thumbs Down* sign as an instant response to a series of short yes/no questions.
2. Before beginning a question or review session, students make *response cards* with content-specific words or symbols written on index cards or similarly sized squares of paper. Information on each card could be numbers, mathematical signs denoting processes, categories, identifying names, or simply the words *yes* and *no*, or the symbols + for presence and – for absence of a quality. Students hold up the appropriate card or card combinations in response to your series of questions.
3. Students use pieces of *dry erase boards* and markers to write brief responses to your questions. At your signal, they hold up the boards for you to see. Large hardware and home improvement stores often have scrap ends from customers' custom cuttings that are free to teachers for the asking. Stores will usually even trim them to size.

These techniques for whole class response are easy and fun for the students. They allow English language learners to participate in a linguistically simple and nonthreatening manner. They get the entire class actively involved and, at the same time, give you immediate feedback about the students' level of understanding.

### Select Question Types

Another strategy to promote participation involves selecting the types of questions you direct to your English language learners. They may be able and willing to respond to questions requiring only short answers. Pattern your questions to them as yes/no, either/or, or one-word response questions.

> Did the South win the Civil War?
>
> Which one is a mammal—a whale or a shark?
>
> Who can give me another example of a mammal?

The drawback of questions such as these is that they are lower-order questions that do not involve much thought processing. Responses to this type of question demand only simple recall of information. To become critical thinkers, students need to engage in processing higher-order questions which require them to explain, analyze, synthesize, and evaluate information. For English language learners, these questions also generally require higher levels of language ability as well. You can get your ELLs involved in more complex thought processing by directing follow-up questions to them:

> Do you agree with Yaset's answer?
>
> Why?
>
> Why not?
>
> Can you add anything to that answer?

### Numbered Heads

An effective way of encouraging student participation involves allowing small groups of students a brief period of time to discuss possible answers to a question you've asked before calling on anyone to answer it. Figure 7.4 explains the structure of the technique known as *Numbered Heads*. This strategy offers extra linguistic support for English language learners at the same time that it reinforces conceptual understanding for all students. It is an excellent technique to simultaneously promote participation and increase student-student interaction as well.

### Watch for Student Readiness

Look closely at your ELL students' faces when you direct a general question to the whole class. Sometimes you can sense that certain students would like to try to answer but can't quite bring themselves to raise their hands. This is a good time to *invite* their participation. Assist their efforts to answer by encouraging them to use visual aids to support their words. Help them by pointing to pictures, places on maps, or words on the chalkboard.

**Numbered Heads**

Seat students in small groups. Within the group, each student chooses a number, 1 through 4 or 5—as many numbers as there are members in the group.

After asking a critical thinking question, allow students a minute or two to discuss the answer. When time is up, ask all the Number 3s, for example, in each group to raise their hands. Call on one of the Number 3s to share the results of the group discussion. Call on the Number 3 person in another group to add more information. Continue until you are satisfied with the completeness of the information. Then repeat the procedure again with the next question.

**FIGURE 7.4. A Novel Way to Increase Student Interaction and Participation**

## *Lower Anxiety*

Feelings of anxiety hamper students' ability to participate and interfere with effective thought processing. You can lower anxiety for your English language learners by giving them extra *wait-time*, the time you give students to think and respond after you ask a question. Your usual wait-time may not be adequate for them because they have not only to think of the answer, but also to process the language of the question and their response. ELLs benefit from wait-times of five seconds for simple questions and as much as ten to twenty seconds for more complicated questions. The sound of silence may be uncomfortable to you at first, but extended wait-times help lower the feelings of pressure and anxiety that often accompany being called on to produce an answer in a new language.

### Give Credit for Trying

Acknowledging incorrect answers with a positive response is another way of making students feel more willing to participate. Try saying one of these with sincerity and a smile when students offer misinformation:

> Good try.
> Almost.
> Thank you for trying.
> Not quite, but you're thinking.
> What an interesting (unusual) way to look at it.

These responses lessen the stigma and anxiety of wrong answers and encourage continued attempts at participation.

### Give Students a Face-Saver

Offering your students a face-saving manner of not answering a question also lowers anxiety levels. It can be accepted practice for students in your class to exercise the option of responding with "Pass", after which you can add, "Fine. We'll get back to you later."

Students can also call on another student for assistance. To make this an effective learning technique, the student you first called on should paraphrase or repeat the information given by the student who assisted in answering the question.

### Repeat, Review, and Summarize

English language learners benefit from repetition of content information. As you teach, ask frequent questions so students can repeat, review, paraphrase, and summarize content. Those who know the material get a chance to shine, and those who don't get the opportunity to hear the information again.

As often as every five or ten minutes, ask appropriate questions:

> So, what did we just cover?
> Who remembers the reasons for _____?
> Who can explain the process we just saw?
> So why was _____ important?

One middle school teacher treated these review questions as a game-like challenge. At any point in the lesson, she would announce, "Quick Check!" The students became instantly alert in anticipation of the question and the opportunity to score bonus points. They loved it—perhaps your students will, too.

# INCREASING STUDENT-STUDENT INTERACTION IN THE CLASSROOM

## Do More Small Group Work

Group work promotes concept acquisition through social interaction. Small groups create a natural setting that encourages the negotiation of meaning in a nonthreatening environment. For English language learners especially, small groups offer the opportunity to use academic language in a meaningful way. ELLs can explore new vocabulary, attempt oral communication, and clarify knowledge through the exchange of information, examples, and comparisons. Many students learn better by negotiating meaning with peers within the safety of small groups.

Student-student interaction also includes pairing students to work together. Partners or buddies act as resources for each other by enhancing each other's understanding, as in the saying *two heads are better than one*. Consider allowing your English language learners to produce a pair product while other students work individually. Students may be able to accomplish together an assignment that neither one of them could complete alone. Think of it as an equation: $1 + 1 = 2$.

Many teachers are reluctant to engage in group work because they worry about loss of control. Following a set of basic rules for group work will maximize your chances for successful group activity in your classroom.

### *Rules for Group Work*

1. Good group work starts by *selecting an appropriate task*. And what exactly is an appropriate task? It is one in which students must work together because each student in the group has only *part* of the information needed to reach the final product. Students must negotiate and cooperate to figure out how to make all the pieces work together as a whole.

    A good way to understand the concept of an appropriate task is by looking at one that is definitely *not*. In this example of an unsuccessful group experience, the teacher tells the students that they are going to work in groups to review material from a content reading. Each student in the group gets a copy of a worksheet with five questions on it along with directions to "work together to answer the questions."

    What happens here? After several minutes of silence, one student asks the others in the group, "So what did you put for Question 1?"

    As one student offers an answer, the others quickly write it down. Why would students work together? The task itself necessitates no negotiation of meaning, no communication or cooperation, no need to exchange of information during this group work session.

Hand out envelopes containing slips of paper, each with different pieces of information in the form of words, phrases, or sentences that students need to arrange. Depending on the type of content to be reviewed, students work together to group items based on qualities or characteristics, arrange items sequentially, or classify items by types and subtypes.

**FIGURE 7.5. An Appropriate Group Task to Review Content**

In contrast to this poor example, Figures 7.5 and 7.6 offer two ideas of appropriate tasks for structuring group work. These types of tasks are challenging for students and widely adaptable for use in content classrooms.

2. Good group work *follows a set of class rules* that have been generated through class discussion before the first group work session takes place. Students can be directed to include rules about staying in seats, using conversational voices, disagreeing politely, and staying on task.

Rules should be on permanent display where they can be referred to if necessary, as a reminder during group sessions. Some strange quirk of human nature makes students less likely to argue with the statement, "You're not following rule number two about using conversational voices," than with the perceived accusation, "Your voices are way too loud."

3. Divide the class into *heterogeneous groupings*. All groups should reflect the general mix in your classroom. In each group there should be diversity of gender, ability, language, and ethnicity. It is well proven that heterogeneous grouping promotes learning for students at all levels of achievement.

4. Introduce the topic and task, and give *explicit directions*. Follow up with a *clarification check* to make sure students know exactly what to do. Use the five-step approach summarized in Figure 7.3 earlier in this chapter in the section Clarifying Comprehension.

5. Give students a *time frame* for completing the task. People of all ages seem to work better under the pressure of a deadline. Allocate the minimum amount

Hand out envelopes with names of people, places, or things on slips of paper. Ask students to group items based on perceived similarities in as many ways as they can. Students must explain the basis for each set of groupings.

**FIGURE 7.6. An Appropriate Group Task to Encourage Critical Thinking**

**1.** Select an appropriate task.

**2.** Set up ground rules for group work.

**3.** Group students heterogeneously.

**4.** Give clear directions.

**5.** Announce a time frame for completion.

**6.** Monitor the groups as they work.

**7.** End with a whole class sharing.

**FIGURE 7.7. Summary of the Rules for Good Group Work**

of time you think the task will take and announce frequently how many minutes remain to complete the work. If students groan about not being able to finish so fast, you can always extend the time as needed.
6. *Monitor the task* by walking around the room as students work. Consider this a golden opportunity to answer student questions and offer individual help.
7. Bring *closure* to group work through whole class sharing. Even if the group work is ongoing, students should report on how the session went and where their group is now. It rewards students' natural curiosity to see the progress and products of the other groups.

If you'd like to do more group work in your classroom, follow these rules (summarized in Figure 7.7) and start small. Build up to big group projects over a period of time. But even before you get to the big ones, you'll see that even small ones bring big results.

## Try Peer Tutoring

Small group work forms an advantageous balance especially in multilevel classrooms. Certain students enjoy the role of peer tutor or peer coach. They can be used to effectively help others who learn more readily by hearing information explained by their peers. The strategy of peer tutoring may also offer a rewarding solution for students who consistently finish individual assignments early and are willing to assist those who need some extra help.

Peer tutoring is a strategy that benefits everyone. The students who are doing the tutoring are reinforcing and expanding their conceptual knowledge through explanation. Those who are being tutored benefit from personalized, one-on-one instruction in a nonthreatening setting. And you, the teacher, benefit from your small cadre of assistants who give you more flexibility to monitor your students' understanding and progress.

### Big Benefits from Small Groups

You may be like many teachers who, for a variety of reasons, just don't do much group work in class even though you know that group work is good. What you may not know is how *very good* group work really is.

The benefits of group work and peer tutoring are enormous—not just for ELLs but for all students. Small group interaction promotes concept acquisition and cognitive growth. It offers an excellent opportunity for students to use academic language in a meaningful way. It allows exchange of questions and clarification of knowledge in a less threatening environment. It personalizes and adds a social element to learning and instruction. It can change students' attitudes toward content and to school in general. It ultimately raises students' feelings of self-confidence. In pair and small group work, one plus one really does add up to more than two.

## A FINAL THOUGHT

Using a combination of these strategies to modify your teaching techniques will facilitate content learning for your English language learners. Your students will move from spectators in your classroom to active participants in the process of their own learning.

CHAPTER **8**

# Adapting Your Personal Teaching Techniques

Have you ever had the experience of trying to talk to someone in a foreign language? You may have had an opportunity to visit a country whose people speak a language you studied in school. Or perhaps you tried to learn a few useful phrases in preparation for a trip. You managed to ask, "Où est la gare?" or "¿Dónde está la playa?" You felt delighted to be understood. And then you got the answer—and poof! the bubble of satisfaction burst. You didn't have the faintest idea where the train station or the beach really was. The words seemed to be coming at you so fast that you couldn't make sense of them at all.

Why do speakers of foreign languages seem to be speaking so fast? It's actually not because of the rate of speech but rather the rate of listening: Nonnative speakers are *slow listeners*. They need extra time to bring meaning to what they're hearing. They need to actively process the incoming language. It is not an easy thing to do especially while trying to pay attention to the flow of new words that continue to be spoken.

Imagine now that these foreign words are not about something simple like the price of a souvenir or the directions to the restroom. Imagine instead that they deal with complex academic concepts in math, science, and social studies classrooms. That is the challenge faced by English language learners in content classes.

## THE DIFFICULTIES OF ORAL ACADEMIC LANGUAGE

The spoken language of academic instruction is difficult for language learners for several reasons. First, oral language is ephemeral in nature. Words, once spoken, are gone. There is no way to rehear them for review.

The second reason is that the nonnative listener takes more time to process the incoming words than the speaker takes to deliver them. Concentrating on the meaning of one spoken sentence interferes with the ability to listen to the next one. Listening is such a complex task that even native speakers have occasional lapses in comprehension in instances like listening to TV news or to radio traffic reports.

The third factor that makes oral instruction difficult for language learners is that English, the language they are trying to learn, is the *medium* through which academic content is delivered. For ELLs, the language itself adds an additional burden of complexity to understanding the content. Understanding academic concepts depends not just on *what* the teacher says, but also on *how* the teacher says it. For ELLs, the *how* can help bring meaning to the *what*.

This chapter deals with strategies to simplify the way you speak when you teach. One section of strategies offers ideas to enhance the clarity of your spoken language. Another is designed to reduce the complexity of your language during oral instruction. The objective of these speech modification strategies is to provide language-sensitive instruction to facilitate the challenge of academic listening for English language learners.

## CHANGE THE PACE OF YOUR SPEECH

### Slow Down

The simplest and most helpful strategy to modify the way you speak is to slow down. Unfortunately, it is not equally easy to do. The goal is to speak at a slightly slower pace, but not so slowly that it feels or sounds unnatural. A good way to slow speech down is to *pause* at natural breaks between phrases or sentences for an extra second or two. Pausing gives ELLs valuable extra time for language processing.

### Enunciate

Another modification to speech is to enunciate your words as clearly as possible. One way to achieve this is to *enhance your intonation* as you speak. Highlight important words by raising or lowering your voice level and your pitch. Giving special intonation to key content words in speaking is the equivalent to underlining, bolding, or italicizing words in writing. Clearly enunciated, well-paced speech with interesting patterns of tonal variation is much more enjoyable to listen to and easier to understand than speech that is rapid and monotonal.

Let's return again to Mr. Elkind, the middle school social studies teacher. On the first day of class, he likes to give his eighth-grade students an overview of what they'll be learning in the course of the year. His introduction, shown in Figure 8.1, is clearly a heavy dose of language for the English language learners in his class. Mr. Elkind needs to pause frequently and emphasize the important content words through rising or falling intonation as he gives this little speech to his class. Compare your ideas of how he should say this to the pattern shown in Figure 8.2.

To demonstrate how effective this strategy is, look at Figure 8.3 listing the boldfaced words, the ones designated for special emphasis, in Mr. Elkind's

This year we'll be studying the significant historical events that led to the development of our nation's traditions. We'll survey American history with a special emphasis on the nineteenth century. We'll first examine in detail the Declaration of Independence and the Constitution because they're fundamental to the history of the United States. Then we'll study topics such as slavery, the Civil War, Reconstruction, industrialization, and the United States as a world power.

**FIGURE 8.1. Mr. Elkind's Course Overview**

"This year . . . we'll be studying the significant **historical events** that led to the development . . . of our **nation's traditions**. . . . . We'll survey **American history** . . . with a special emphasis on the **nineteenth century**. . . . We'll **first** examine in detail the **Declaration of Independence** . . . and the **Constitution** . . . because they're **fundamental** to the history of the United States. . . . **Then** . . . we'll study topics such as **slavery**, . . . **the Civil War**, . . . **Reconstruction**, . . . **industrialization**, . . . and the United States as a **world power**."

**FIGURE 8.2. Mr. Elkind's Overview Revisited**

historical events
nation's traditions
American history
nineteenth century
first
Declaration of Independence
Constitution
fundamental
then
slavery
the Civil War
Reconstruction
industrialization
world power

**FIGURE 8.3. Getting the Message from Only the Boldfaced Words**

introduction. Reading through the list of just those words *alone* gives you a pretty good idea of the message the passage will convey. You really can make an important difference in comprehension for your English language learners by speaking more slowly through enhanced pausing and intonation.

## SIMPLIFY YOUR SPEECH

Native speakers use speech patterns that differ greatly from patterns used in writing. Simply put, we speak differently than we write, and it is all perfectly normal and correct. Speakers tend to use familiar words in short simple sentences. Often they use phrases instead of complete sentences. Speakers lose their place and backtrack, or they repeat themselves. They make false starts and use extraneous words as fillers or spacers. They regularly use contractions and merge words together.

Understanding the teacher's spoken academic language is a complex task for English language learners. Teachers can ease the task by making minor adaptations to their normal speech patterns.

### Limit Use of Contractions

All fluent English speakers contract words when speaking. It is one of the normal differences between spoken and written English, and also a salient difference between language learners and native speakers.

For English language learners, contractions are a source of misunderstanding. Words like *they're* and *it's* are easily confused with their other forms—*there/their* and *its*. There is also the issue of the two ways of contracting *it is not*—do *it isn't* and *it's not* really mean the same thing? Many ELLs do not connect the spoken *should've*, which sounds like *should of*, with its written form, *should have*. And almost every listener has experienced the difficulty of hearing the difference between *can* and *can't*.

You can help your ELLs by using the full form of these and other contracted words—*they are, it is, it is not*, and *cannot*—as often as you can remember. The uncontracted forms help ELLs not only by making the meaning more apparent, but also by slowing down your rate of speech.

### Use Fewer Pronouns

English language learners can bring meaning to spoken language more readily by hearing more nouns and fewer pronouns. Although it may sound a bit strange or stilted to you, try to repeat names and other nouns more frequently than you might normally. Pronouns involve some extra language processing and can slow down comprehension. Even native speakers occasionally become confused when *it* or *they* is used too many times.

## Use Simple Words and Be Consistent

Varying your word choices through synonyms and colorful words may make speech sound more interesting, but for English language learners, it adds another source of confusion. Oral academic language can be simplified for ELLs by using simple, high-frequency words instead of unusual ones and by repeating known words instead of using synonyms. Spoken words that are familiar and recognizable to ELLs allow them to focus more clearly on the concepts you are trying to convey. The more consistent your terminology and word patterns, the more readily your ELLs can process the content.

Consistent wording of oral directions for assignments and activities is another area of importance for English language learners. Teachers tend to be unaware that they are using different words to give the same set of directions, as in

Circle the word that best describes . . .

Draw a circle around the best word choice for . . .

Find the word that best fits each question and then circle it.

Choosing one word pattern to communicate these directions and using it on a regular basis is a helpful strategy that simplifies oral input for ELLs.

The words you speak in class should also be consistent with the words and phrases used in the students' textbooks. A brief examination of the words used to give directions or to discuss a topic in the textbook can help you decide which words and phrases to use in presenting and discussing the material. When you believe that directions written in the text seem unclear or overly complicated, like those in Figure 8.4, explain them through paraphrase and discussion. For ELLs, maintaining consistency of the words they hear in

---

**If the textbook says:**

Evaluate the following expression for the given value of the variable.

$A + 5 =$          for $A = 2$; $A = 6$; . . .

**Paraphrase to:**

(*Good*)   Find $A + 5$ when $A = 2$.

Find $A + 5$ when $A = 6$.

(*Better*)   If $A = 2$, then $A + 5 = ?$

If $A = 6$, then $A = 5 = ?$

---

FIGURE 8.4. Simplify Complicated Directions from the Textbook

class and the words they read in their textbooks is another strategy to facilitate comprehension.

A recent trend in some school districts is to require teachers to use updated terminology to express traditional ideas. Modern jargon calls an essay *an extended constructed response* and a paragraph *a brief constructed response*. Students no longer take multiple-choice tests; now their tests involve *selected responses*. And they don't compare books; instead they make *text-to-text connections*. Use jargon if you must, but be sure that all your students know what the new words really mean.

## Become Aware of Idiomatic Language

Idioms and figurative speech make speech colorful and interesting. Language learners feel they are learning the "real English" when they learn idioms, and perhaps they are. Native speakers use them liberally in speech. Unfortunately, idioms and figurative speech also confuse ELLs because the meaning of the individual words does not reflect the actual meaning of the whole message.

Teachers use figurative language to get their students' attention. A teacher, wanting to check students' understanding of new material, might begin the question session with an enthusiastic opener like, "OK . . . I'm going to pitch some practice questions. Let's see who can hit a homerun here!" It definitely adds an element of fun, but the ELLs in this classroom are likely to respond by looking around the room for a baseball and bat.

It is not always possible to avoid using idioms and figurative speech, nor would you want to. They personalize and flavor speech, and often are a means of injecting interest and humor. Developing an awareness of the idioms and figurative speech you use as you speak allows you the opportunity to paraphrase or explain them in a simple way.

## Simplify Your Sentence Structure

A final way to modify your speech is to keep sentences short and simple in structure. Teachers often bring to class articles or books to supplement information in the students' textbooks. They read aloud passages that were meant to be read silently and processed slowly. The long, complex sentences of written text make them difficult to process orally. Look at this textbook sentence:

> The Civil War, which took more American lives than any other war in our history, divided the people of the United States, so that in many families, brother fought against brother.

You can facilitate the listening comprehension for your ELLs by simplifying the sentences and paraphrasing the wording to this:

---

The Civil War divided the people of the United States. It even divided families. In many families, brother fought against brother. More Americans died in the Civil War than in any other war in American history.

---

## ENHANCE YOUR WORDS

### Use Gestures

Have you ever heard people say that they couldn't talk if their hands were tied behind their backs? Americans, and speakers of many other languages as well, use their hands to make gestures that supplement their words. Hand gestures, along with facial expressions and body language, make speech easier to understand. It is the difference between learning through audio- or videotape, and getting information in person or over the telephone.

In classroom instruction, English language learners will become more involved if you make oral language a visual experience. Be sure to make ample use of the gestures and facial expressions that come naturally. When you tell your students, "There are three important things to remember," hold up three fingers for your students to see. Continue using one, two, and three fingers as you explain each piece of information. Point prominently to your first finger when you review by asking, "What was the first thing we discussed?" Students form a visual picture that helps them retain the information.

Take advantage of any pictures or objects in the classroom that you can use to illustrate a particular word. Try pantomime to help explain a new or difficult term. It is a surefire way of getting the attention of all your students.

### Use Visuals and Graphics

Support your words with graphic representation. Use the "chalk-talk" approach: Write key vocabulary words and phrases on the board or on an overhead transparency as you speak them. Seeing a word in writing at the same time as you speak it facilitates comprehension for ELL students.

Try to get in the habit of using graphic organizers as a regular part of your teaching. Graphic organizers contextually embed oral language. They help English language learners understand vocabulary, concepts, and relationships in a linguistically simplified way.

Incorporate pictures, photos, maps, graphs, tables, or anything else you may have on hand to help illustrate the meaning of your words. Draw a picture of an object—even stick figures and rough sketches are helpful. Refer to them as you talk. Remember the adage: *One picture is worth a thousand words.* For language learners, this is a primary principle.

Supplement class lectures and discussions with filmstrips, slides, videotapes, DVDs, and CD-ROM programs. Encourage students to find and share content-appropriate Websites on the Internet.

Bring in *realia* to explain and interest your students. Realia are authentic, real-world objects that illustrate a concept in ways that allow students to make meaningful connections to their own lives and to the world outside the classroom. Using bank deposit slips and check registers for a unit on banking or working with copies of actual floor plans to calculate square footage motivates student learning. Suggest that students contribute their own realia. It may be an interesting cultural experience for you and all your students.

## Demonstrate Your Words

Show your students how to find an answer or solve a problem through demonstration and modeling. Take your students through a step-by-step process to explain how to reach the end result. For each step, do a think-aloud to demonstrate *why* you choose to do it a certain way and why you choose *not* to do it other ways. Ask aloud the questions you would normally ask yourself silently as you show the steps you take. It is important to *not* make it seem too simple. Students need to realize that thinking, adjusting, and readjusting are a natural part of the learning process. Figure 8.5 shows some appropriate classroom applications of this strategy.

## Be Dramatic

Make your lessons memorable by hamming them up. Dramatize, emote, role-play, pantomime—have a good time! Doing these things gives your students tacit permission to be dramatic as well. Groups of students may enjoy

**How to** locate information to answer a question

**How to** highlight important information

**How to** select the main idea and supporting details

**How to** sequence information

**How to** summarize information

**FIGURE 8.5. Use Think-Aloud Demonstration to Show Process**

staging mini-reenactments of events or acting out imaginary dialogs between historical or scientific figures. Students will remember the material and probably you, too.

Creative approaches to instructional delivery are important for English language learners. ELLs need to learn not just by listening, but also by watching and doing. Adding visual elements to speech helps to contextualize the oral language of instruction. Remember Cummins's Quadrants in Chapter 2, Figure 2.1? Using strategies that move oral instruction from Quadrant IV to Quadrant III makes it easier for ELLs to understand concepts and content.

## START SMALL, BUT START NOW

Changing highly ingrained speech habits and mannerisms is something of a challenge. The first step in the process, and perhaps the most difficult, is becoming aware of what you actually do.

A good way to start thinking about the way you use oral language in your classroom is to record—on audio- or videotape—a lesson you teach. As you replay it, listen closely to your use of language, and select one or two areas you would like to work on. Choose the strategies that you think would help, and begin to incorporate them into your patterns of oral instruction. When those feel comfortable, try working on others, one or two at a time.

Each modification you add enhances the clarity of your oral instruction for your English language learners. You may find that these strategies facilitate learning for all the students in your class.

# PART III

# Strategies for Assessment

# CHAPTER 9

# Adapting Classroom-Based Assessments

Recent emphasis on school accountability has turned the spotlight on student assessment. The focus of attention is now on the annual standardized tests that determine whether students have met state and local standards. However, the importance of classroom assessment practices should not be overlooked. Well-written teacher-made tests can maximize learning and ultimately raise performance levels on high-stakes tests.

---

### Case Study—A Final visit to Mr. Elkind's Classroom

Mr. Elkind, the middle school social studies teacher, has given the issue of assessment, especially as it relates to his English language learners, a great deal of thought. Mr. Elkind gives frequent quizzes and short tests to his students, so that they always know exactly where they stand. In all his tests, he seeks to balance basic, factual multiple-choice questions with essay questions that involve more complex relationships and higher levels of critical thinking. He clearly understands why his ELLs don't do well on the essays; he knows these questions are heavy in language demand. What puzzles him is why they also don't do well on the multiple-choice sections. These questions seem easier because they test only simple factual knowledge, and students have only to recognize the right answer.

Grading is also a problem for Mr. Elkind. Although many of his English language learners do poorly on his exams, he hates to write grades of D or F on their papers. But what grade should he give them? It seems like a double penalty to give them a low grade in social studies content knowledge just because they lack the English language skills to express that knowledge. And he believes that giving them the low grades they consistently earn on his tests will make them feel like failures; poor grades will only lower their self-esteem and motivation even further. On the other hand, if he gives them a higher grade, is that fair to the students who really earned those higher grades? It's a real conundrum.

---

Mr. Elkind's situation raises some essential issues about assessment. At the core of these issues is this question: How can teachers evaluate English language learners' mastery of subject matter in a way that separates content knowledge from English language knowledge. As Mr. Elkind discovered, using the same tests for all the students in the class is not the answer.

## ESSAY QUESTIONS, MULTIPLE-CHOICE QUESTIONS, AND LANGUAGE DEMAND

Teachers often create tests that combine essay and multiple-choice (M-C) questions, much like those of Mr. Elkind. And they encounter the same difficulties because the language demand of the tests is beyond the proficiency level of their ELL students. Simply stated, essay questions pose a heavy *writing* load, and multiple-choice questions pose a heavy *reading* load.

### Essay Questions

Formulating responses to essay questions is a multistep process combining content knowledge and English language *writing* skills. Students must first understand what the question is asking. Next, they must sort through mental files to retrieve appropriate content information, and then organize it to address the question. The final step, and quite possibly the most difficult for ELLs, is to structure that content information into a cohesively written answer. The fact that some native English-speaking students struggle with essays offers an insight into the degree of challenge this format presents to English language learners.

### Multiple-Choice Questions

The multiple-choice question format requires English language *reading* skills generally beyond the level of ELL students. Well-written multiple-choice questions demand critical analysis of four or more options in order to select the best answer. Options that are long or worded with subtle distinctions like the examples in Figure 9.1 cause language confusion that prevents ELLs from demonstrating their content knowledge. For ELLs, a test of several pages of multiple-choice questions presents a formidable reading task.

Multiple-choice tests that offer students combinations of option choices like those shown in Figure 9.2 increase the reading load even further. Questions like these require students to first read and comprehend the information presented in the options, then match the correct facts to the question, and finally weed out the one, two, three, or even all four incorrect choices. Combining option choices in multiple-choice questions simply adds an additional level of confusion for many students, not only the ELLs.

---

1. The Battle of Antietam was important because
   a. the South regained all of Virginia but Stonewall Jackson was killed.
   b. Confederate troops abandoned Kentucky and increased Grant's determination to win.
   c. Richmond was saved from capture and northern forces retreated.
   d. the Confederate retreat gave Lincoln the occasion to issue the Emancipation Proclamation.

2. The people known as "Copperheads" were
   a. policemen exempt from fighting to maintain order in northern cities.
   b. miners from the North who formed a fighting unit in the Union Army.
   c. men who deserted shortly after being paid for enlisting in the Confederate Army.
   d. Democrats demanding an immediate armistice and peaceful settlement of the war.

3. The North and South had different opinions about tariffs. Choose the statement that is true.
   a. The North wanted high tariffs because it helped sell tobacco and cotton in foreign countries.
   b. The South wanted high tariffs because it helped factories make better goods.
   c. The North wanted high tariffs because it made the price of foreign goods higher.
   d. The South wanted high tariffs because it was good for foreign trade.

---

**FIGURE 9.1. Typical Multiple-Choice Questions on the American Civil War**

Multiple-choice tests are challenging for English language learners for still another reason: The format is unique to the American school system. The majority of students from other countries have had no experience with this common type of test before their arrival in U.S. classrooms. Lack of familiarity with the format makes multiple-choice tests even more difficult for English language learners.

## The Pitfalls of Multiple-Choice Tests

Multiple-choice question tests have become the preferred test format for one reason: They are easy to score. It is their primary advantage, and with so many demands on teachers' time, it is an important one. This type of test, however,

Changes in energy consumption in the United States during the past 100 years are due to

        (a) population growth.
        (b) industrialization.
        (c) modernization.
        (d) medical advances.

A. Both (a) and (b).
B. Both (b) and (c).
C. All but (d).
D. None of the above.
E. All of the above.

**FIGURE 9.2. Combining Option Choices Is Confusing**

has many inherent disadvantages and pitfalls. While there are only a few rules for writing good multiple-choice questions, there is an almost infinite number of ways to write bad ones.

High-stakes standardized tests generally avoid many common pitfalls because they are created and field-tested by professional test makers. Classroom teachers have neither the time nor the expertise to create tests at the same level of sophistication. Multiple-choice tests created by teachers for classroom use are often flawed.

Making up a set of good multiple-choice questions is difficult and time consuming. The foremost problem with teacher-made M-C tests lies in writing questions that assess students' deep conceptual understandings. It is easy to create items that check basic lower-order knowledge of factual information such as names, dates, and definitions. However, trying to write higher-order questions—those involving critical thinking and problem-solving skills—may produce options (Figure 9.3 shows the terminology of the parts of a M-C question) that are unnecessarily long, confusing, silly, or illogical.

To be a true test of content knowledge, distractors must seem like reasonable choices and appeal to those who don't know the correct answer. For questions that test factual knowledge, teachers have available an abundance of good option choices. There is never a shortage of dates, names, places, and definitions to serve as attractive distractors to the correct answer. Testing the type of knowledge shown in Figure 9.4 is using the multiple-choice format to its best advantage.

However, even in its best application, there remains the issue of backwash—the effect that tests have on learning. Because M-C questions require

| | |
|---|---|
| **Stem** | 1. A glacier may be defined as |
| **Options** | a. turbulent water moving down a river.<br>b. a huge mass of ice or snow that moves slowly over land.<br>c. small particles of material moved by water or wind.<br>d. the process of moving particles of rock grinding away other rock. |
| **Correct response** | **Option b** |
| **Distractors** | **Options a, c, and d** |

**FIGURE 9.3. Parts of a Multiple-Choice Question**

(e) A nation with a population that is not increasing is

a. Peru.
b. Guatemala.
c. Sweden.
d. Kenya.

**FIGURE 9.4. Multiple-Choice Questions Best Assess Simple Factual Knowledge**

students to simply recognize the correct option when they read it, this type of test often has a negative effect on the way students process information. In the world outside the classroom, those who are asked a question (other than "May I take your order?") are not often given choices from which to select a correct response. They are expected to *produce* an answer.

There are additional pitfalls to teacher-made multiple-choice questions. The wording of the stem may point to the correct option, as shown in Figure 9.5, or the options themselves may point to the correct choice, as in Figure 9.6. The distractors may not appear reasonable enough choices to actually be chosen as an answer, one example of which is shown in Figure 9.7.

Questions that include the word *never* or *always* may penalize the more knowledgeable students who think of exceptions that mislead them from selecting the intended choice. Information in one test question may inadvertently offer a clue that helps answer another question on the test. Guessing and cheating are factors as well. In sum, multiple-choice tests may not be the best indicator of students'—*all* students—true knowledge.

A network of all the feeding relationships in an ecosystem is called a

        a. ecological pyramid.
        b. energy chain.
        c. food web.
        d. energy web.

Options **a, b,** and **d** can be eliminated because they would require the stem to end with **an** instead of **a,** leaving **c. food web** as the only grammatically correct choice.

**FIGURE 9.5. Wording in the Stem May Point to the Correct Answer**

Of the following, the factor most likely to result in a decrease in the size of a specific population is

        a. improved medical care.
        b. increased food availability.
        c. famine.
        d. industrialization.

The three distractors, **a, b,** and **d,** are all positive factors. Only the correct choice, **c. famine**, is negative.

**FIGURE 9.6. Options Can Highlight the Correct Choice**

Wild animals are considered domesticated when they

        a. enjoy being with people.
        b. are toilet trained.
        c. eat burgers and fries.
        d. are taught to work for human beings.

**FIGURE 9.7. Unreasonable Distractors Don't Distract**

So now to return to the core question: How can ELL students be tested in ways that allow them to show their content knowledge while minimizing their dependency on English language knowledge? The solution is to modify test techniques and to offer alternative assessments. Simple changes can make big differences in student performance on tests.

## MODIFY TEST TECHNIQUES

### True/False Questions

The English language learners in your class will be more able to demonstrate their content knowledge when you create a parallel test for them by replacing the stem and options of M-C questions with a linguistically simplified format. True/false questions are one way to do this. For each M-C question, substitute a complete sentence using the M-C stem plus any one of the options. When the statement is false, require students to correct the word or phrase that is in error.

### Identification Questions

In certain situations, identification questions can be used advantageously in place of the M-C format. When the content of a test assesses the learning about two or more contrastive concepts, as in Figure 9.8, you can change the usual M-C format of individual questions with stem and options to a format in which simple statements must be labeled with the concept they describe. Identification questions of this type can cover a large amount of information while significantly lowering the amount of reading involved. This format has the additional teacher advantages of being easy to write and simple to score.

### Completion Questions

Completion questions, using the M-C stem but replacing the options with a space or blank lines, are another means of linguistically simplifying M-C tests. Lowering the reading and language demand allows English language learners to focus their efforts on content. Compare the tremendous difference in reading demand when the three questions from Figure 9.1 are presented in a completion format, shown in Figure 9.9. In conjunction with the completion questions, ELL beginners can additionally be offered a content word or phrase bank as a supplementary aid.

The *cloze* technique extends and interrelates a series of completion type questions. In a cloze format, the teacher composes one or more paragraphs in which key content words or phrases have been deleted. In their places are blanks for the student to fill in. Figure 9.10 shows the use of a cloze passage to assess comprehension of the circulatory system in the human body. Again, true ELL beginners could use a word bank to assist them.

**Forest Biomes**

Write the letter of the forest biome to which each statement below applies.

     C = Coniferous Forests

     D = Deciduous Forest

     R = Rain Forests

_____ 1. Location: temperate zone

_____ 2. Location: subarctic regions of North America, Europe, Asia

_____ 3. Location: tropical zone

_____ 4. Location: climate with 4 different seasons

_____ 5. Trees have buttressed trunks

_____ 6. Trees are triangular shaped

_____ 7. Trees produce seeds

_____ 8. Trees shed leaves seasonally

_____ 9. Trees have needles

_____ 10. Trees have shallow root systems

_____ 11. Soil: poor, acidic

_____ 12. Soil: thin, nutrient poor, nutrients recycled back into trees

_____ 13. Soil: rich, fertile

_____ 14. Examples: cypress, balsa, teak, mahogany

_____ 15. Examples: maple, oak, beech, ash, hickory, birch

_____ 16. Examples: hemlock, fir, spruce, cedar

_____ 17. Biome with the greatest biodiversity

**FIGURE 9.8. Identification Questions Lower the Amount of Reading**

Giving English language learners true/false, identification, and completion questions in place of multiple-choice puts the focus where it belongs—on content, not on reading ability. These types of questions offer the additional benefit of avoiding many of the pitfalls of M-C testing. And, from the teacher's perspective, they are easier to write than M-C questions and almost as fast to score.

1. The Battle of Antietam was important because _____

   _____.

2. "Copperheads" were people who _____

   _____.

3. The North wanted _____ (high or low?) tariffs because

   _____.

**FIGURE 9.9.  Completion Questions Put the Focus on Content**

**Circulation**

Circulation is the pumping of blood around the body. The

_____ is the main organ of the circulatory system. It never

rests. It _____ and _____ in a regular, even motion,

about _____ times a minute. It makes the blood travel around

your body bringing _____ to muscles and other parts of the

body.

Tubes that carry blood around the body are called _____.

There are three types of tubes that carry blood. Each type has a different

job to do. Arteries _____ (what do they do?). Veins

_____ (what do they do?). And capillaries _____

(what do they do?).

Blood is made of four main parts. The largest part of blood is called

_____. Its job is to _____. The three other parts

of the blood are (1) _____, whose job is to

_____; (2) _____, whose job is to

_____; and (3) _____, whose job is to

_____.

**FIGURE 9.10.  The Cloze Technique Takes Completion Questions to the Next Level**

## Use Graphics to Express Knowledge

Essay questions can also be linguistically simplified. In place of sentences and paragraphs, English language learners can use visuals and graphics for their response. ELLs can demonstrate their understanding of content with graphic organizers, T-notes, sequenced pictures, labeled diagrams and maps, or any of the other ideas presented in Chapter 6.

## Bend the Rules

Modify some of your regular rules for communication while testing. For example, allow ELLs to use a *bilingual dictionary* to clarify words they may be unsure of in English. Encourage ELLs to seek clarification of specific test parts they don't understand.

   *Answer questions* that don't influence or give away content. *Substitute a synonym* for an unknown word. *Paraphrase directions* that ELLs don't understand. Consider having a bilingual student *translate the directions* for a complicated test into the students' native language. It might even be feasible to *translate the questions* themselves. In addition to any of these modifications, you could also *allow rewrites and test corrections* to improve grades and demonstrate more complete understanding.

   Use *flexible timing* for testing your ESOL students. Think about dividing the test into several shorter sections and giving each section separately. Consider *shortening the test* by selecting only concepts of primary importance. The second question in Figure 9.1 (see page 113) is an example of a question that could be comfortably eliminated.

   Another means to shorten the test and decrease the reading load as well is to *reduce the number of options* offered as choices to each multiple-choice question. This has the additional advantage of giving ELLs practice with this question type without overwhelming them. In combination with any of these other strategies, you could also allow ELLs to use their textbooks during the test. For beginners, you might even consider noting a page number next to each question.

   A seemingly radical idea is to *pair* two ELL students to take a test. Working together may allow them to complete more of an exam than either one of them could do individually. And finally, if time allows, you could give sections of a test as an *individual oral exam.* Oral language may be an easier modality for ELLs to convey content knowledge.

## DON'T "TEST" AT ALL!

"Not testing at all" doesn't *really* mean not giving any tests. It means using alternative assessment techniques and measures in place of, or as a complement to, more traditional forms of tests. It is a productive way of evaluating English language learners' content knowledge.

## Performance-Based Assessment

Performance-based assessments allow students to demonstrate their content knowledge through concrete examples, including writing samples, projects, visuals and graphics, oral reports, presentations, and portfolios. All performance-based assessments are based on a set of criteria that teachers make clear to students in advance of assignments. Explaining the standards—scoring rubric, checklist, point distribution, for example—that will be used for assessment and showing examples of excellent work increase students' ability to meet the criteria. English language learners, in particular, benefit from seeing models, knowing the teacher's expectations, and understanding the criteria used for evaluation.

## Portfolios

Portfolio assessment has gained popularity among teachers and school administrators in recent years. Teachers work together with their students to formulate selection standards and evaluation criteria.

Portfolios empower students by enabling them to choose the items that will be evaluated. Students can demonstrate mastery of content through a wider variety of measures than paper and pencil tests would allow. Portfolio collections document growth of both content knowledge and language skills over a period of time. Used in conjunction with other forms of evaluation, portfolio assessment offers students an alternative means of demonstrating their developing understanding.

## Information Journals

Like portfolios, information journals (also called content journals or learning logs) can be used as a valid means of evaluation. For ELL students who keep them on a regular basis, information journals will show progress over time. Examples of learning logs are shown in Chapter 5, Figures 5.18 and 5.19. The more highly structured the journals are—using, for example, the K-W-L-H format discussed in Chapter 7, Figure 7.2—the easier they will be to evaluate. Students may be extra motivated to work on their information journals knowing that they are being used for assessment purposes.

## Self-Assessment and Peer-Assessment

Self-assessment and peer-assessments are useful to supplement and complement other types of evaluation. Teachers can create individual *checklists* that students complete reflecting their personal feelings about comprehension of text or topic, contributions to class or group work, and areas of strength, weakness, and/or improvement. Figures 9.11 and 9.12 show examples of checklists to which items can be added or changed as needed. Students can offer additional

| Textbook: Chapter 12 | ☹ | 😐 | ☺ |
|---|---|---|---|
| **WEEK OF** _____ <br><br> I understood the reading. <br> I highlighted the text. <br> I used a dictionary. <br> I worked with a friend. | | | |

**FIGURE 9.11. Self-Assessment Checklist I**

| Textbook: Chapter 12 | Usually Not | Sometimes | Almost Always |
|---|---|---|---|
| **WEEK OF** _____ <br><br> I understood the assigned reading. <br> I highlighted the text. <br> I made note cards. <br> I made vocabulary cards. <br> I participated in class discussions. <br> I asked for help when I was unsure. | | | |
| I also want to tell you that _____ <br><br> _____ <br><br> _____ <br><br> _____ | | | |

**FIGURE 9.12. Self-Assessment Checklist II**

1. The concepts I understood were _____.

2. The concepts I didn't understand were _____.

3. I think I improved in _____.

4. I think I need more improvement in _____.

5. I need special help with _____.

6. The kind of help I need is _____.

**FIGURE 9.13. Open-Ended Self-Assessment**

information about their self-assessments when teachers add an extra column or include a section at the bottom, as in Figure 9.12, for explanatory comments. An even more individually expressive format for self- and peer-assessment involves completing a set of *open-ended questions,* as shown in Figure 9.13.

Teachers who routinely use self- and peer-assessment at the end of each chapter or unit, or at the end of each week, month, or grading period, find that it helps to open and maintain a line of communication with their ELL students. Students' insightful input can often help teachers find more effective techniques and approaches to facilitate comprehension. Students feel empowered by contributing to their own evaluations. There are few assessment techniques as positive as this one.

## THE ISSUE OF GRADING

You will not share Mr. Elkind's grading dilemma (at least, not to the same degree) when you modify your regular tests and use alternative means of assessment. Because these assessment strategies offer more opportunity and wider means for English language learners to show what they know, you will have more accurate feedback to use in grading them. Beyond this, there are several other ways to make grading fairer to your English language learners.

- **Focus on content.** Try focusing on content only instead of the language used to express that content knowledge. Look for key content words in short answers and give at least partial credit, even if the whole answer is not completely comprehensible to you.
- **Focus on progress.** Give grades that reflect the student's own progress rather than grading ELLs in comparison to the rest of the class. An asterisk following the grade could denote that you are using an alternative

grading system. Including some positive comments will make ELLs feel more successful, even if their actual grade is low.

- **Give second chances.** Consider allowing ELLs the opportunity to retake a test, to hand in a second draft, or to correct their assignments. Encourage peer correction through collaboration before ELLs submit their work. Partner or small group editing meetings will have a positive effect on grades.

Evaluation combines grading modifications with test modifications and alternative assessment strategies produce a more accurate picture of your ELLs' actual content knowledge. Your language learners can show what they know and earn grades that better reflect their understanding. You are offering them the opportunity to begin to experience academic success.

# CHAPTER 10

# Meeting State Standards

Ever since school districts adopted standardized curricula, teachers have been faced with the issue of how to cover all the topics in one school year. The dilemma has always been one of depth versus breadth—more time on fewer topics, or less time on more topics. Teachers felt torn between conflicting beliefs. On the one hand, covering fewer topics in greater depth allowed opportunities to approach subject material in creative ways that could increase students' interest and motivation. On the other hand, teachers also believed that they had a responsibility to expose their students to all topics in the curriculum to prepare them, at least minimally, for topics they would be expected to know in the next years.

The issue of depth versus breadth is made even more complex for today's teachers who have to deal with state standards, benchmarks, and high-stakes tests. State boards of education have developed standards that outline in excruciating detail what students are expected to know and be able to do in the major subject areas. Because state accountability tests are directly linked to the standards, teachers feel themselves under intense pressure to cover these standards in the course of a school year. If this is a challenge with the *native* English-speaking students in their classes, can they possibly meet those standards with their English language learners? And if not, then what?

These are valid questions. The reality is that English language learners cannot and should not be expected to learn the same amount of content as their native-speaking peers. But ELLs decidedly *can* and *will* learn some of it. It is the teacher's task to decide which standards, concepts, topics, and skills are the important ones for their ELLs to focus on. Those you choose should be core concepts that are individually interesting and cognitively challenging. Some guidelines and practical considerations may help you in the selection process.

## CHOOSING CONCEPTS AND TOPICS FOR ELLs

### Core Concepts

Take a close look at the standards, concepts, unit topics, and subtopics in your curriculum. It will be obvious that they have not all been created equal. Some standards encompass high-level thinking skills and broad concepts; other

| Math | Science | Social Studies |
|---|---|---|
| equality | adaptation | culture |
| operations | energy | liberty |
| equivalence | force | change |
| symmetry | matter | exploration |
| number systems | properties | rights/responsibilities |

**FIGURE 10.1. Some Core Topics in Math, Science, and Social Studies**

standards are more narrowly based on separate, discrete skills and information. Topics, as well, can be viewed in a similar manner. Certain topics in your curriculum may be considered *core* topics, those that recur and are conceptually extended in each successive year of schooling. Concepts like those shown in Figure 10.1 form the foundation of knowledge upon which the understanding of more advanced complex information, ideas, and relationships will depend.

You can best help the ELLs in your classroom today by selecting and concentrating on only the core topics, skills, and standards that they will be expected to know and do in the academic years that follow. Keep in mind that English language learners are in the process of learning a new language at the same time they are trying to learn content. Focusing on core concepts for your ELLs does not lower expectations: It simply repositions them at a more realistic level.

## Interesting Topics

Inherent interest in a topic is a natural motivator to learning. Students learn better—more quickly and in greater depth—when they are motivated. Students generally are interested in topics that relate to previous personal experiences, to prior learning, and/or to real-world connections. Linking standards, topics, and skills to the particular interests of students in your class makes learning meaningful to them, and meaningful content is more easily understood and retained.

There is no doubt that you *will* have to make some content choices for the English language learners in your classes. You can facilitate their learning by selecting topics that individually interest them and, at the same time, maintain a high level of cognitive challenge, as discussed below.

## Challenging Topics

Topics selected for study need to maintain a high level of academic challenge. English language learners will not benefit in the long run from a watered-down curriculum. Thoughtful selection of content involves combining cognitively demanding topics and concepts with activities that require the use of higher-level thinking skills.

To achieve this, focus on content *depth* rather than *breadth*. Turn your English language learners into class specialists by having them concentrate their attention on a narrow section of content instead of trying to cover all the information that the rest of the class will learn. Figures 10.2 and 10.3 list appropriate subtopics for your ELLs specialists to study. Figure 10.4 includes suggested types of assignments as well. ELLs can be working on their expert topics at their own pace independently, in pairs, or in small groups, producing an example such as the graphic shown in Figure 10.5, while you continue your lessons with the class. They will have learned a great deal in the process about content, concept, and language. You also create the opportunity to show your ELLs in a positive light when you "call on the experts" to share knowledge as their topics arise during class discussion.

Inviting ELL students to become specialists in a narrow field of study is a pedagogically sound approach to learning. Long-term retention of knowledge is dramatically increased when learning is focused on the principle of *learn more about less*. Students who merely learn facts for the test often retain the information only until the test is over. Memorized lists are quickly forgotten, while information that has been thoroughly researched is often long remembered.

Combining depth of study with choice based on interest will give your English language learners a solid chance to learn challenging material. You will

| Unit | Expert Focus |
|------|--------------|
| Freshwater resources | Water pollution |
| Ocean motions | Currents |
| Weather factors | Precipitation |
| Energy resources | Fossil fuels |

**FIGURE 10.2. Topics for Class Specialists in Earth Science**

| Unit | Expert Focus |
|------|--------------|
| Human anatomy | Skeletal system |
| Human physiology systems | Circulatory system |
| Sense organs | Sense of sight |
| Mammals | Mammal habitats |

**FIGURE 10.3. Topics for Class Specialists in Life Science**

| Unit | Expert Focus | Assignment Type |
|------|--------------|-----------------|
| The Constitution | Amendments | Time line |
| | The seven articles | Graphic representation |
| | Separation of powers | Graphic representation |
| | U.S. government v. system of government in ELL's native country | Venn diagram |
| The Civil War | Life in the North v. life in the South | Venn diagram |
| | One battle: Antietam | Map; outcome graphic |
| | One general: Lee or Grant | Time line |
| | The two generals compared | Venn diagram |
| The growth of the West | Railroads | Time line, map |
| | Mining | Map; products |
| | Effects on Native American tribes | Graphic representation |
| The Progressive Era | Rise of unions | Time line |
| | Reforms for women | Time line |
| The Great Depression | Causes of the Depression | Graphic representation |
| | New Deal program summary | Graphic representation |

**FIGURE 10.4. Topics for Class Specialists in American History**

have offered them the best possible means of becoming actively and effectively involved in their own learning.

## Practical Topics

The final guideline to consider is practicality. If you are deliberating among several topics that appear equal, take a practical approach and select those you believe may be easier to make comprehensible to English language learners. Certain standards and concepts are more concrete and demonstrable in content and process. They will be linguistically easier for ELLs to understand because they lend themselves to simple graphic representation. They allow you to more readily scaffold instruction by using the strategies discussed in Part II of this book.

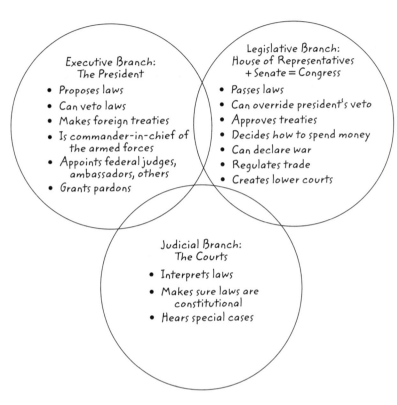

**FIGURE 10.5. A Specialist's Report—The Three Branches of Government**

## THE IDEAL AND THE ACTUALITY

Wouldn't it be wonderful if all your students could meet all the standards and learn everything in your curriculum? Of course it would, but that is in an ideal world. The actuality, of course, is different—some of your students will do it all and some will not. English language learners, with good reason, will be in the group that will not.

The reality is that you must make curricular choices. Attempts to cover the entire required range and breadth with your ELLs may well result in little actual learning and a great deal of confusion. You can help them so much more by focusing on content, concepts, and standards that are important, foundational, cognitively challenging, interesting, and practical. You will be giving them the gift of academic success.

# CHAPTER 11

# Preparing for High-Stakes Tests

Teachers in every state of the United States face the twin issues of accountability and high-stakes testing. Performance results on standardized or state-designed assessment instruments affect decisions about promotion, curricular tracking, and graduation for students and, in many states, teacher, school, and district ratings and funding as well. Poor showings may result in the imposition of corrective actions ranging from schoolwide restructuring to providing students with alternative school choices. Never before have test stakes been so high.

With accountability and testing as important as they now are, teachers and administrators have become deeply involved in preparing students for successful outcomes. They have developed new programs and innovative approaches for improving the performance levels of their students—their native English-speaking students, that is. For better or worse, however (and there really are two sides to this issue, though that is beyond the scope of this text), English language learners, too, must face these tests.

In the past, potentially low-scoring English language learners were simply excused from high-stakes testing. Exclusion, at this time, is no longer a general option. It is now mandated that almost all ELLs must participate in the same statewide assessment instruments as their native-speaking peers.

It seems unrealistically optimistic to expect ELLs to achieve the same level of performance as their English-speaking peers, but it would be equally pessimistic to believe that they are destined to fail. Teachers can maximize the performance potential of their ELLs on yearly state-mandated tests by using a combination of strategic approaches throughout the school year: Incorporate into your daily procedures a variety of the instructional strategies presented in Part II to facilitate content comprehension; use the classroom assessment strategies discussed in Chapter 9 to give students ongoing practice in test taking; explicitly teach test-taking skills; and finally, ensure that the most appropriate and beneficial test accommodations are being made available to English language learners. These last two strategic approaches will be the topics of this chapter.

## TEST-TAKING STRATEGIES

### Format Familiarization

English language learners, first and foremost, need to become familiar with the format of multiple-choice (M-C) tests, as this test type is not widely used outside the United States. The process of reading the stem and option choices (parts of M-C questions are labeled in Chapter 9, Figure 9.3), eliminating the incorrect options, and then bubbling in the chosen response on a separate answer sheet may completely bewilder ELLs. Frequent practice with this type of test will sharpen their skills and make them more comfortable with M-C test design.

Start English language learners on a positive testing path by *thinking small*. Introduce language learners to the M-C format by offering only two option choices per question. Increase the number of options to three shortly thereafter.

A second way to familiarize ELLs with M-C questions is to give them two parallel tests. Use any of the linguistically simplified forms of tests questions discussed in Chapter 9 so that ELLs can demonstrate their actual content knowledge. *At the same time*, give them a set of M-C questions that exactly parallel the questions on the first test. For example, students could see a true/false question in parallel with a two-option M-C question as in Figure 11.1, or a fill-in-the-blank question with a three-option M-C question, as shown in Figure 11.2. By comparing the stem, options, and actual correct answer on the M-C questions to the same question written in the simplified formats, students will begin to make sense of the M-C process. To clarify their understanding even further, students can analyze each of the M-C distractors and circle the word or phrase that makes it incorrect.

The two strategies, offering two or three option questions and giving parallel tests, work well in combination. With continued practice, students will feel more able to work with standard four-option questions.

---

T  F    A glacier may be defined as a huge mass of ice or snow moving slowly over land.

A glacier may be defined as

  a. turbulent water moving down a river.
  b. a huge mass of ice or snow that moves slowly over land.

---

**FIGURE 11.1. Parallel Test Questions: True/False with Multiple Choice**

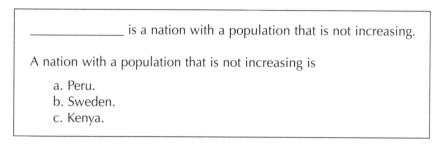

_____ is a nation with a population that is not increasing.

A nation with a population that is not increasing is

    a. Peru.
    b. Sweden.
    c. Kenya.

**FIGURE 11.2. Parallel Test Questions: Fill-in-the-Blank with Multiple Choice**

## Predictable Patterns and Phrases

When English language learners understand the design of the multiple-choice format, practice sessions can extend to familiarizing students with common word patterns of test directions. Written directions on standardized or statewide tests often differ from those students are accustomed to hearing in class or reading in their textbooks. Word patterns of directions for a given task can also vary from one test to another. It may not be apparent to ELLs that the two sets of directions in Figure 11.3, for example, are asking them to do the same thing. Familiarization with the variations in word patterns will allow ELLs to focus their linguistic efforts on finding answers to the questions instead of trying to figure out what to do with the questions themselves.

## Test-Taking Skills

At this point, English language learners can join the rest of the class when you teach test-taking skills. All students will benefit from learning testing strategies to "improve the odds," as, for example, knowing in advance whether wrong answers are penalized or not. In tests that assess penalties for wrong answers,

Choose the word or group of words that means the same, or about the same, as the underlined word. Then mark the space for the answer you have chosen on your answer sheet.

Bubble in the letter of the word or phrase that is closest to the meaning of the underlined word.

**FIGURE 11.3. Same Task, Different Directions**

students should be encouraged to guess only if they can eliminate two of the options. If there are no penalties for guessing, the best strategy is to answer all questions. However, students need to know that choosing one letter—either option b or c, as these more frequently contain the right answer than either option a or d—and using it consistently throughout the test offers the best statistical odds for a correct guess.

## More Tests Make Better Test-Takers

English language learners become better test-takers through repeated practice. It is a good idea to establish a pattern of twice monthly mini-assessments. Shorter tests, given more often, allow ELLs to focus on understanding smaller amounts of material. They serve as grade indicators; students know how they are doing at all times throughout the grading period. They prevent the surprise of failure at the semester's end. They allow students multiple opportunities to improve their grades. They let teachers know whether students have a good grasp of concepts or whether reteaching, review, and/or additional individual services are needed.

Perhaps most important of all, frequent tests prepare students for bigger exams. Each test and quiz increases students' familiarity and comfort level with understanding and following directions, choosing correct responses, and using appropriate test-taking strategies. Practice may not make ELLs perfect, but it *will* make them better.

## TESTING ACCOMMODATIONS

High-stakes standardized tests now mandate the inclusion of English language learners. The benefit of including ELLs' test results in school accountability data is that their instructional needs can no longer be minimized or ignored. However, those test results may more accurately reflect their English language proficiency than their actual content knowledge. To address this very real difficulty, four types of testing accommodations may be offered to English language learners: accommodations in presentation, response, setting, and timing. Teachers who are aware of these test modifications and use them to their best advantage can maximize the performance potential of their English language learners.

## Accommodations in Presentation

Teachers may offer clarification to their ELLs in several different ways. Directions can be read aloud, repeated, paraphrased, and/or simplified. If state law allows, directions may even be translated into students' native languages and recorded in advance by qualified teachers, parents, or other community volunteers.

Students may also request clarification during test administration. Teachers should answer questions that enhance ELL students' comprehension of the question; providing the teacher's response will not affect the student's answer on the test. The unusual vocabulary in the math problem shown in Figure 11.4, for example, might interfere with ELLs' ability to demonstrate their actual math knowledge. Figure 11.5 shows the problem reworded and simplified. Nothing mathematical has changed—only the linguistic ability needed to understand what the question is asking. Test results will more accurately reflect ELLs' content knowledge and skills when teachers explain, rephrase, or simplify non-content-related vocabulary, synonyms, idiomatic phrases, and cultural references.

---

A stable manager had a 78.3-foot length of braided leather line to use to replace the fraying reins on his horse bridles. Which equation could be used to find $L$, the number of lengths of rein measuring 3.7 feet that could be cut from the 78.3 feet?

    A.  $78.3L = 3.7$

    B.  $78.3 = 3.7L$

    C.  $L = (3.7)(78.3)$

    D.  $\dfrac{L}{78.3} = 3.7$

---

**FIGURE 11.4.  A Linguistically Difficult Math Problem**

---

Which equation could be used to find $L$, the number of lengths of string measuring 3.7 feet that could be cut from a length of string measuring 78.3 feet?

    A.  $78.3L = 3.7$

    B.  $78.3 = 3.7L$

    C.  $L = (3.7)(78.3)$

    D.  $\dfrac{L}{78.3} = 3.7$

---

**FIGURE 11.5.  Same Problem, Linguistically Simplified**

Giving teachers the opportunity to conduct a linguistic preview of test questions may reduce the need for clarification during actual testing sessions. Items such as overuse of synonyms, unfamiliar terminology, and embedded complicated questions can be rewritten in simplified form and included as part of the test, either in the test booklet itself or as a separate handout.

## Accommodations in Response

The most valuable modification in the response category is to allow English language learners to use reference aids such as bilingual dictionaries and glossaries. Students can use commercially published editions or they can bring to the test preapproved vocabulary journals or dictionaries that they have created throughout the school year.

Other suggested modifications in response may be more difficult to implement. For example, ELLs may be offered the option of marking their answers directly in the test booklet. This, however, makes scoring difficult and may be a costly option as well. Two even less likely modifications are to allow ELLs to respond in their native language or, for large language groups, to offer assessments in the students' native language. Both of these options present almost as many problems as they attempt to solve.

## Accommodations in Setting

Modifications in this category include administering standardized tests to ELLs in a separate classroom and in small groups. Together, these accommodations offer ELLs a more comfortable test-taking environment and lower their levels of test-related anxiety.

## Accommodations in Timing

Giving ELLs extra time to complete tests is a reasonable and workable modification. Because ELLs must spend additional time decoding and deciphering the language of the test in order to demonstrate their content knowledge, it seems fair to extend the time they have to do this. Adding an additional ten or fifteen minutes to a forty-five minute test segment would compensate ELLs for language difficulties and produce a more accurate assessment of their content achievement levels.

## Recommended Combinations of Accommodations

Effective accommodations balance the needs of English language learners and the resources of test administrators. Combining modifications that are practical and relatively easy for schools to accommodate with ones that offer ELLs maximum benefits produces a short list of recommendations:

- Test ELLs separately in small group settings.
- Give ELLs additional time to take the test.
- Allow ELLs use of bilingual reference aids.
- Simplify directions, word usage, and long, complicated questions.
- Encourage ELLs to seek clarification during the test.

This seems to be a viable combination of accommodations. School resources will not be unduly burdened, and test outcomes will more accurately reflect English language learners' content knowledge and skills. It is a win-win situation—students, teachers, and schools will all benefit from the results.


## THE CHALLENGE

Yes, English language learners in content classes present a challenge to their teachers—first to facilitate understanding of subject-area content for them, and then to create instruments and opportunities that accurately evaluate the learning that has taken place. The strategies of instruction and assessment detailed in this volume have given you the means to help you meet that challenge.

Start by choosing strategies that appeal to you and integrate them into your instructional routines. Add more strategies on a regular basis. Experiment with them—try them out with the whole class, not just the ELLs. Integrate different types of strategies—learning strategies, textbook strategies, assignment strategies, instructional strategies, teaching strategies, and assessment strategies. Evaluate those that work well and those that appear less effective. Eliminate the ones that don't seem to be productive for your group. Discuss them with your colleagues; share ideas and applications. Keep trying. You, like your students, will be encouraged by the rewards of success.

And you *will* be rewarded. By choosing to use these strategies, you point your English language learners toward the path of achievement. With each small accomplishment, they begin to build their academic self-confidence and personal self-esteem. To you, their teacher, goes the credit for making these students successful participants in the academic environment that is such an important part of their daily lives.

Yes, it is a challenge. But it is an exciting and rewarding challenge—one that is well worth embracing.

# Strategies

# Glossary of Common ELL Acronyms

| Acronym | Meaning |
| --- | --- |
| **BICS** | Basic Interpersonal Communication Skills |
| **CALP** | Cognitive Academic Language Proficiency |
| | |
| **LEP** | Limited English proficient |
| **NEP** | Non-English proficient |
| **PEP** | Partially English proficient |
| **FEP** | Fluent English proficient |
| **NES** | Non-English speaker |
| **LES** | Limited English speaker |
| **FES** | Fluent English speaker |
| | |
| **EFL** | English as a foreign language |
| **ELL** | English language learner |
| **ESL** | English as a second language |
| **ESOL** | English for speakers of other languages |
| **TESOL** | Teaching English to speakers of other languages |
| | |
| **ESP** | English for specific purposes |
| **IEP** | Intensive English program |
| **NNS** | Nonnative speaker |
| **NS** | Native speaker |
| **LM** | Language minority |
| **LCD** | Linguistically and culturally diverse |
| **CLAD** | Cross-cultural, language, and academic development |

# Student Resources: English Language Aids

## For Beginners

### *Student Dictionaries*

*Oxford Picture Dictionary for the Content Areas*, Oxford University Press, 2000
> Also available in English/Spanish version.

*Word by Word Picture Dictionary*, Pearson Education, 1993
> Also available in eight bilingual versions: English + Spanish, Japanese, Chinese, Korean, Portuguese, Russian, Vietnamese, Haitian Kreyol

*Vox Spanish and English Student Dictionary*, McGraw-Hill, 1999

## For High Beginners and Low Intermediates

### *Student Dictionary*

*Longman Basic Dictionary of American English*, Pearson Education, 1999
> All three levels of the *Longman Student Dictionary* series use the Longman Defining Vocabulary, the 2000 most common English words, to ensure that all entries are easy to understand.

## For Intermediates

### *Student Dictionary*
*Longman Dictionary of American English*, 3rd ed., Pearson Education, 2002

### *Thesaurus*
*Longman Essential Activator*, 2nd ed., Pearson Education, 2002

### *Dictionary of Idioms*
*Longman Pocket Idioms Dictionary*, Pearson Education, 2002

## For High Intermediates and Advanced

### Student Dictionary
*Longman Advanced American Dictionary*, Pearson Education, 2001

### Thesaurus
*Longman Language Activator*, Pearson Education, 2002

### Dictionary of Idioms
*Oxford Idioms*, Oxford University Press, 2001

### Collocation Dictionaries
*Oxford Collocations*, Oxford University Press, 2002
*LTP Dictionary of Selected Collocations*, Language Teaching Publications, 1999

# Teacher Resources: Suggestions for Further Reading

## About Instructional Strategies

Cary, Stephen (2000). *Working with Second Language Learners: Answers to Teachers' Top Ten Questions*. Portsmouth, NH: Heinemann.

Chamot, Anna Uhl, Bernhardt, S., El-Dinary, P. B., and Robbins, J. (1999). *The Learning Strategies Handbook*. White Plains, NY: Pearson Education.

Chamot, Anna Uhl, and O'Malley, J. M. (1994). *The CALLA Handbook: Implementing the Cognitive Academic Language Learning Approach*. White Plains, NY: Pearson Education.

Daniels, Harvey, and Semelman, S. (2004). *Every Teacher's Guide to Content-Area Reading*. Portsmouth, NH: Heinemann.

Diaz-Rico, L. T., and Weed, K. Z. (2002). *The Cross-Cultural, Language, and Academic Development Handbook: A Complete K–12 Reference Guide* (2nd ed.). Needham Heights, MA: Allyn & Bacon.

Echevarria, Jana, Vogt, M., and Short, D. J. (2000) *Making Content Comprehensible for English Language Learners: The SIOP Model*. Needham Heights, MA: Allyn & Bacon.

Freeman, Yvonne S., Freeman, D. E., and Mercuri, S. (2002). *Closing the Achievement Gap: How to Reach Limited-Formal Schooling and Long-Term English Learners*. Portsmouth, NH: Heinemann.

Gibbons, Pauline (2002). *Scaffolding Language, Scaffolding Learning: Teaching Second Language Learners in the Mainstream Classroom*. Portsmouth, NH: Heinemann.

Richard-Amato, Patricia A, and Snow, M. A. (2004). *Academic Success for English Language Learners: Strategies for K–12 Mainstream Teachers*. White Plains, NY: Pearson Education.

Walters, Therea (2004). *Teaching English Language Learners: The How-To Handbook*. White Plains, NY: Pearson Education.

## About Culture

Helmer, Sylvia, and Eddy, C. (2003). *Look at Me When I Talk to You: ESL Learners in Non-ESL Classrooms*. Portsmouth, NH: Heinemann.

Igoa, Cristina (1995). *The Inner World of the Immigrant Child*. New York: St. Martin's Press.

## About Assessment

O'Malley, J. Michael, and Valdez-Pierce, L. (1996). *Authentic Assessment for English Language Learners: Practical Approaches for Teachers*. White Plains, NY: Pearson Education.